Patterns for Patches

Patterns for Patches

A Selection of Patchwork,
Appliqué and Quilting Patterns

by Deborah Brearley

Hodder & Stoughton

SYDNEY AUCKLAND LONDON TORONTO

First published in 1987
by Hodder & Stoughton (Australia) Pty Limited
2 Apollo Place Lane Cove, NSW 2066

National Library Cataloguing-in-publication entry.

Brearley, Deborah
   Patterns for Patches
   Bibliography
   ISBN 0 340 42235 1
   1. Patchwork — Australia 2. Patchwork — Australia —
   Patterns 3. Quilting — Australia — Patterns 4.
   Applique — Australia 1. Title.
746 46041 0994

Design by Derrick Stone
Pen drawings by Moira Laidlaw
Pattern drawings by Deborah Brearley
Quilt photographs by Mike Fisher
Typeset by Savage Type Pty Ltd, Brisbane
Printed in Singapore by
Kyodo-Shing Loong Printing Industries Pte Ltd

Available to the Craft retail trade through
C & A Craft International
49 Karnak Road
ASHBURTON 3147

Preface

After 'Patches of Australia' was published, I realised that a large group of patchworkers had not been catered for — those 'allergic' to pattern and template drafting. To many, especially those new to the craft, the process may seem a very daunting task. I enjoy the designing, planning and drafting processes, but most patchworkers do not share my enthusiasm. So full-size templates in two block sizes — 30 cm (approximately 12 inches) and 20 cm (approximately 8 inches) — have been included in this book.

Another group has been catered for with some new patterns: those people who like the 'creepy crawlies' of the wildlife world. Many of us befriended a blue tongue lizard when we were younger, treating it with eggs and bananas. The reader will notice that the appliqué and quilting patterns include butterflies, moths, lizards and, for those particularly fond of birds of prey, a black shouldered kite. I have left the snakes and spiders as a personal challenge for those with the greatest passion for 'crawlies' to draft their own patterns at this stage.

Except for the butterflies, which have been produced at slightly larger than life-size, the birds and animals have been presented approximately life-size, as layout has permitted. Check the descriptions for full details regarding each pattern.

This book has three parts. The first is a section which explains and illustrates a number of processes by which the patterns can be explored. It explains and discusses how patterns can be changed and developed as part of the process of designing a quilt. The second part explains how the patterns are used and made into templates ready for cutting and sewing. The final section presents to the reader full size patterns in two sizes — all the reader has to do is trace and sew — there is no tedious pattern drafting or enlarging.

I hope that this book will enable a greater number of people to use the patterns of our flora and fauna, some of the most beautiful and inspiring features of our environment.

Deborah Brearley
June 1987.

For our children's children: may they have a quilt heritage that reflects their country.

Butterfly and wattle blossom

Contents

Acknowledgements

Thank you to the many people who have contributed to the making of this book:

Firstly to Ken and Ryan for their tolerance and patience, living in a household revolving around patchwork thoughts and paraphernalia, especially during the preparation of this book.

To the ladies who kindly tested and made some of the quilts illustrating this book: my sister Jennifer; my mother Anna Hughes; patchwork friends Dot Caple, Barbara Day and Jenny Agnew; the Duck Ponds Patchwork and Quilting Group, Lara; the American Patchwork Tour ladies who made quilts to be presented to groups in America.

To the ladies who loaned their work for the exhibition of samplers and quilts illustrating the development of the patterns, held in March 1986 in the Blackwood Street Gallery, part of the Meat Market Craft Centre of Victoria. Some of the work from this exhibition illustrates the use of the callistemon, eucalyptus blossom and Sturt's desert pea patterns.

To Mum and Dad Brearley, Jenny West and Stuart Miller, native plant enthusiasts; Trevor Pescott, naturalist; and Larry and Dawn Davies, orchid enthusiasts, for the loan and use of transparencies from their collections.

To the people who so willingly shared their gardens, specialist books and time, allowing me to photograph specimens and to discuss the 'finer details' of our flora and fauna.

To the Royal Melbourne Zoo Education Service for the yellow tailed black cockatoo and the bearded dragon transparencies.

Exploring the Patterns

Sulphur crested cockatoo

The 'colour, cut and paste' technique

This is a very simple process by which the block patterns can be explored and developed and a quilt top designed. A small scale block of the desired design is drawn up a number of times.

If the design is not symmetrical, then also draw up a reverse or mirror image of the block — this will increase the number of design possibilities. A few block outlines can be photocopied to save time. Colour the blocks with coloured pencils or felt tipped pens in the appropriate colours, keeping the colour scheme simple at this stage. Before cutting out the blocks, put a mark of identification on each one — this is especially important when reverse images are used, because they can simply be labelled 1, to indicate pattern number or 1R, pattern reverse. The blocks can easily be confused once they are cut apart, especially if you are using blocks which are very similar, like the wattle patterns, illustrated.

When all the blocks have been marked for easy identification, coloured in and cut out, start to arrange them on a work table and experiment with the many different placements. When you are happy with a design you have developed, paste the blocks down onto a piece of paper. A piece of graph paper is preferable, as the grid lines can be used to paste up the design squarely, or if spaces are to be left between blocks or if the blocks are to be offset, then the lines can be used to advantage. The process can be repeated using this pasted-up design as a starting point for more complex designs.

After pasting up the design, photocopy it; then you can experiment with different colour schemes. The wattle pools quilt on page 57 is designed using this process.

Use the wattle patterns 1 and 2 on page 11 and their reverse images to try out this process of design development. You will be surprised at the number of variations you discover.

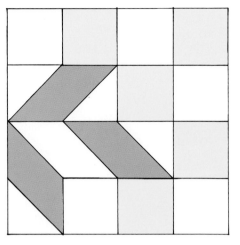

Wattle pattern 1

4 x 4 units

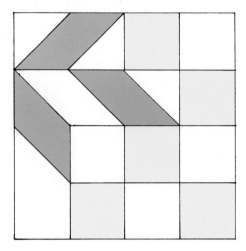

Wattle pattern 2

4 x 4 units

Patterns 1 and 2 are only slightly different, but when four of the one pattern are set together the secondary design is quite different for each pattern.

Make a copy of pages 12, 13 and 14 with wattle blocks (patterns 1 and 2). Colour them, and mark them for identification. Cut them out and paste them onto the grid presented on page 14, to try the 'colour, cut and paste' method of pattern exploration and development.

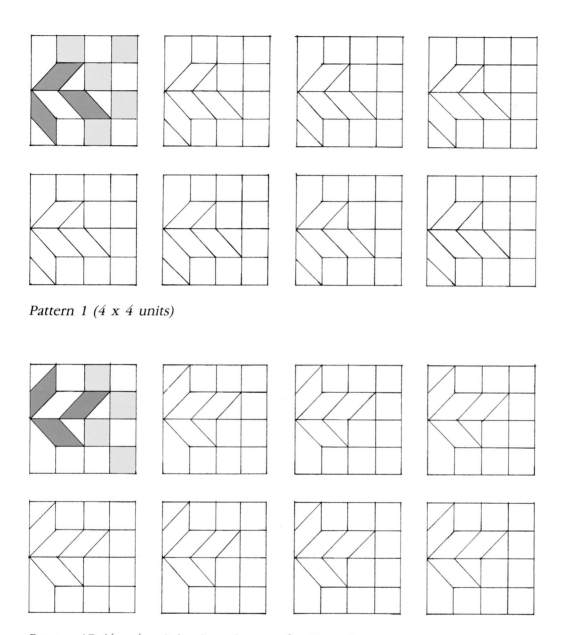

Pattern 1 (4 x 4 units)

Pattern 1R (4 x 4 units) mirror image of pattern 1

Permission is granted to photocopy
pages, 12, 13 and 14 for
the 'colour, cut and paste' technique.

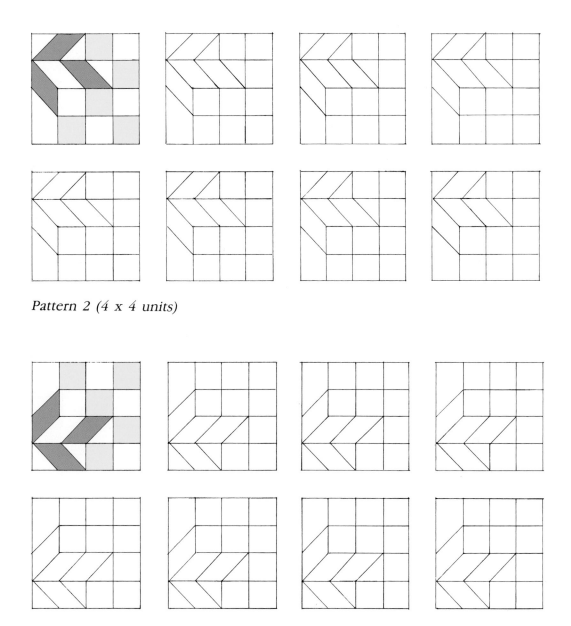

Pattern 2 (4 x 4 units)

Pattern 2R (4 x 4 units) mirror image of pattern 2

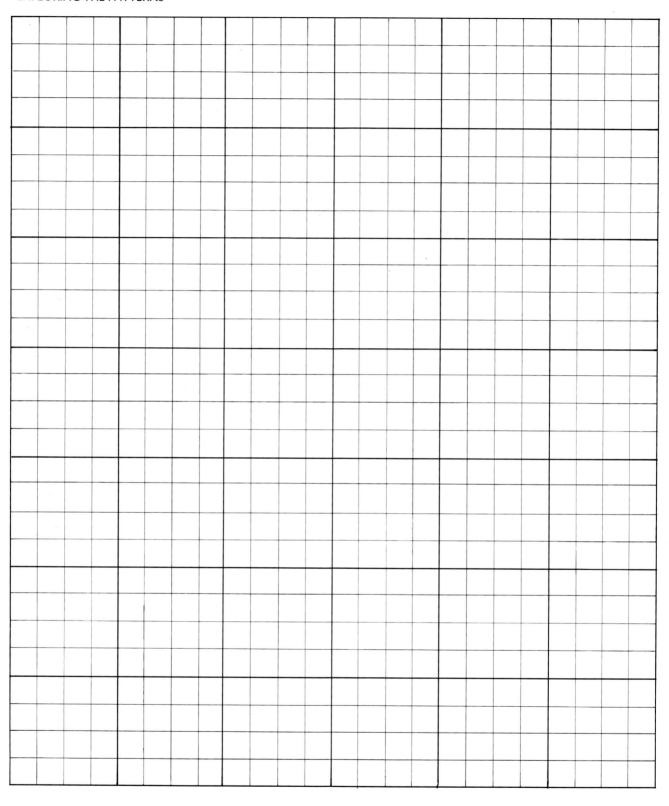

Use this grid as a foundation for pasting on coloured blocks when trying the colour, cut and paste technique of pattern exploration.

WATTLE MEDALLION

This quilt was designed using the 'colour cut and paste' technique. It is a replica of a quilt that was designed and made to be presented to the American quilting group in Huntsville, Alabama who hosted a group of Australian quilters on tour.

CONSTRUCTION:
Hand pieced and quilted.

MEDIA:
Printed and plain cottons.

SIZE:
110 cm × 110 cm.

MAKER:
Mae Bolton.

Developing secondary designs

The blocks illustrated in Figure A are secondary designs — they are blocks that have been developed by arranging four blocks of either, and/or wattle patterns 1, 1R, 2 and 2R, using the 'colour, cut and paste' technique. They resemble, but are quite different from, the original block. The number of blocks that can be 'discovered' in this way is almost endless. Try to make each of the blocks illustrated on the left-hand side of Figure A(i), using the 'colour, cut and paste' technique.

The impact of colour placement

The use and placement of colour in a block can greatly alter the overall appearance. In fact, it is sometimes very difficult to determine that two blocks coloured differently are the same structurally. This is illustrated in Figure A(ii), the secondary wattle blocks, and in Figures B(iii) and (iv), illustrating the development of the secondary designs using a banksia block.

Figure A (i)   *Figure A (ii)*

The impact of colour placement

Banksia pattern (4 x 4 units)

Figure B(i)

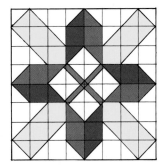

Banksia pattern (8 x 8 units)

Figure B(ii)

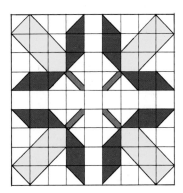

Banksia pattern, repeated four times, separated by lattice strips (9 x 9 units)

Figure B(iii)

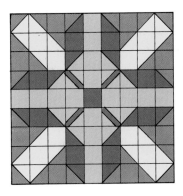

Banksia pattern, repeated four times, separated by lattice strips. This is the same as the above arrangement but by manipulating the colour placement of the background shapes, a completely new block has been developed. (9 x 9 units)

Many of the patterns can be explored in this way. It is especially effective with diagonal arrangements of the motif within the original block, e.g. eucalyptus patterns.

Change the colour of this block to reds and pinks to portray a callistemon.

Figure B(iv)

WATTLE AND SULPHUR CRESTED COCKATOOS

The border was designed using the 'colour cut and paste' technique. This quilt was made as a group project to be presented to a group of quilters in Greensboro, North Carolina, U.S.A. who kindly hosted the group when they visited there.

CONSTRUCTION:
Hand Pieced, hand quilted.

MEDIA:
Printed and plain cottons.

SIZE:
110 cm × 110 cm.

MAKERS:
Pieced by the America Patchwork Tour ladies 1986.
Quilted by Cynthia Hess.

Expanding the basic block modules

Patterns can be explored by repeating the basic block modules over a grid system which extends beyond the bounds of a small or regular number of units.

Eucalyptus blossom

Patterns can be developed by taking the basic shapes which make up the original block and expanding the design into horizontal and/or vertical arrangements like the one illustrated.

A complete quilt top could be designed in this way. The patterns developed are more fluid and have a greater resemblance to the actual species being depicted.

Blocks which are based on the same sized units can also be interlocked, eucalyptus blossom patterns could be used in conjunction with each other to build up secondary designs similar to the one illustrated on page 21.

Experiment with the 'colour, cut and paste' technique previously outlined, using the wattle blocks.

Blocks of different patterns can be interlocked in the same way as long as the unit size is identical, e.g. wattle blocks with eucalyptus blossom and/or waratah blocks etc.

Eucalyptus blossom pattern 2 (4 x 4 units)

An illustration of a design expanded
into horizontal and/or vertical
arrangements as described on page 20.

Combining different block patterns

Blocks of different patterns can be interlocked as long as the unit size of the grid is the same. To maintain the scale of each species in relation to each other, for example the wattle in relation to the size of the gum blossom and waratah, give careful consideration to the quilting designs. Instead of quilting each wattle square with one circle to give the feeling of form to the flower, the quilting of four smaller circles would visually reduce the scale of the yellow square when a shadow is cast by the quilting stitches. The dotted lines in the diagram suggest possible quilting stitches, which, when used, give form and detail to the flowers and leaves. Use these quilting accents along with outline quilting of the motifs.

Use the 'colour, cut and paste' technique to initiate designs. Parts of the blocks can be deleted and/or overlapped so that the overall design loses the formality of the original block units and the 'new' design is more fluid.

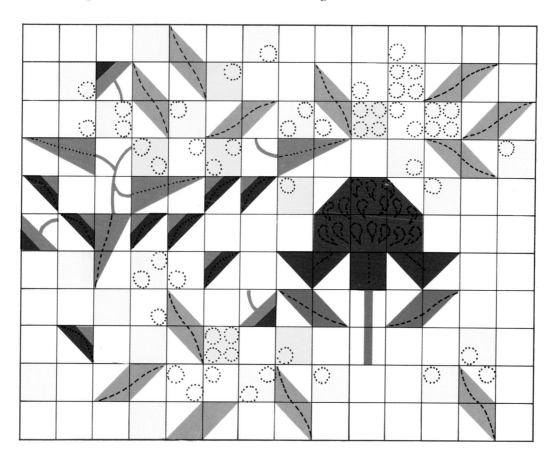

Introducing curves to the pattern grid

Very interesting blocks can be developed by introducing curves to the block pattern. When drawing up a pattern to make the templates some of the diagonal and vertical construction lines can be replaced by a curved line. This line can be drawn with drawing instruments — french curves, flexi curves or less formally, you can use egg cups, plates, or cups as your tools.

Note that the grid system is still the basic structure of the block — the intersecting lines are the points to which the curve is drawn.

Callistemon   5 x 5 units

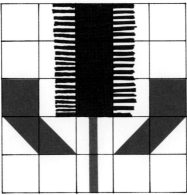
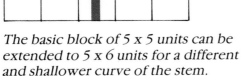

The basic block of 5 x 5 units can be extended to 5 x 6 units for a different and shallower curve of the stem.

The line drawing illustrates the template shapes for the 6 x 5 unit pattern. By dropping the leaf shape down one grid unit, the construction of the top flower unit is a lot simpler than the flower unit in the 5 x 5 unit pattern.

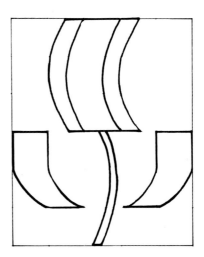

6 x 5 units
Callistemon pattern with curved templates is on pages 24 and 25
Block size 24 cm x 20 cm

Callistemon pattern with curved templates

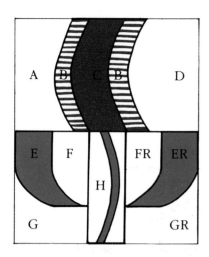

Size 24 cm x 20 cm

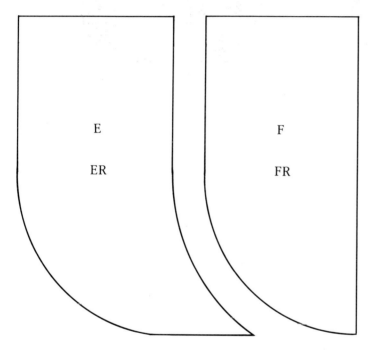

E
ER

F
FR

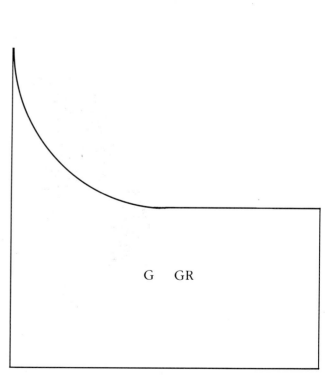

G   GR

Templates for blocks

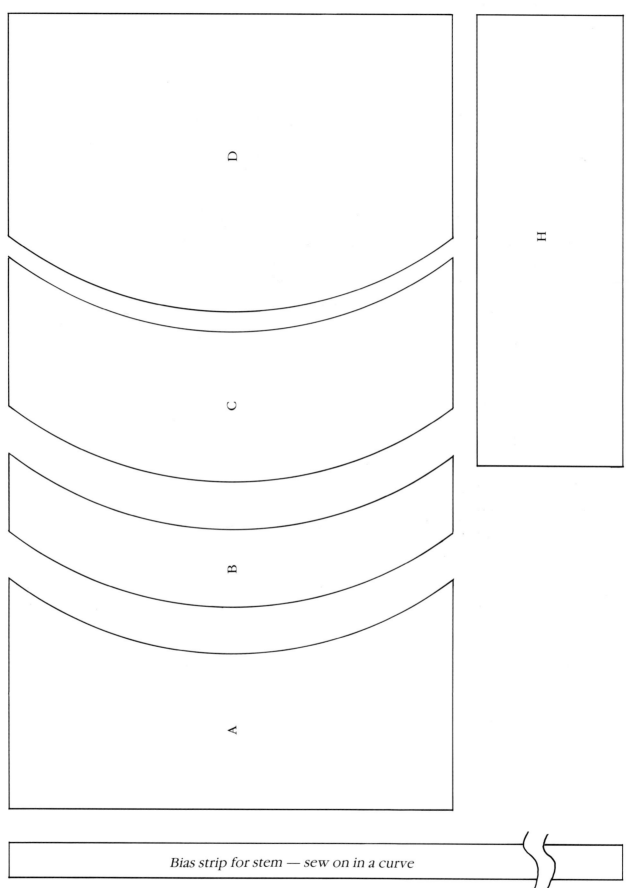

D

C

B

A

H

Bias strip for stem — sew on in a curve

This template is correct width but when making up the design cut a longer bias strip than indicated on this page.

Introducing curves to the pattern grid

Banksia   5 x 5 units

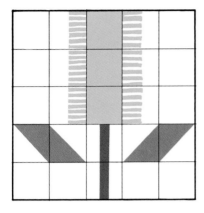
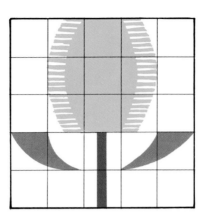

This block could also be used to illustrate the callistemon

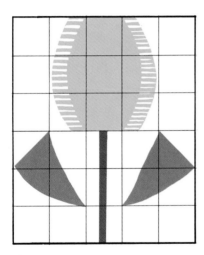
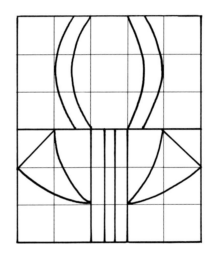

6 x 5 units

Introducing curves to the pattern grid

Eucalyptus blossom   3 x 3 units

Convex and concave curves can be used in conjunction with each other in the one block.

Combining pieced, appliqué and quilting motifs

Pieced blocks can be used to make borders to frame appliqué or quilted motifs. Remember that parts of a quilting design can be used very effectively, for example leaf and flower units have been used separately for quilt motifs for the koala family quilt (page 29).

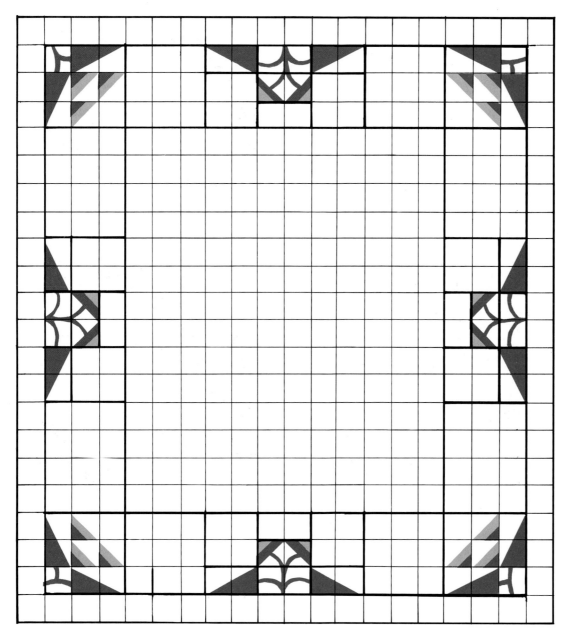

Quilt   22 x 20 units

This quilt border could easily be adapted for a larger size quilt by repeating the side motifs the number of times required to bring the quilt up to the desired size

Combining pieced, appliqué and quilting motifs

The eucalyptus blossom border has been used in conjunction with the koala appliqué patterns.

Koala family quilt

22 x 20 units

If a grid size of 5 cm is used, then the quilt will measure 110 cm x 100 cm, and the quilt will have the same proportions as the illustration when used in conjunction with the koala appliqué pattern.

Combining pieced, appliqué and quilting motifs

Butterfly and eucalyptus blossom quilt

16 x 16 units

The pieced units are the same as the ones used for koala family quilt but they have been used over a smaller number of units. This arrangement could be used as the central medallion for a quilt with outer borders based on the same pieced blocks but repeated over a greater number of units, similar to that of the koala family quilt.

Combining pieced, appliqué and quilting motifs

Black shouldered kite quilt

16 x 16 units

The border is the same as the previous one but colours have been placed so that the secondary design, the curved corners, has been emphasised.

If a grid size of 4 cm is used for the pieced eucalyptus blossom units, the arrangement will have the same proportions as the illustration when using the juvenile black shouldered kite appliqué pattern.

Adapting blocks to depict other flora species

You will notice that elements of these patterns are common to flowers already depicted in block patterns. Explore these patterns using the 'colour, cut and paste' technique.

Hakea

This pattern depicts the species of hakea which has its leaves and flowers growing up the stems, e.g. *Hakea cucullata* (red flowers) or *Hakea ferriginea* (flowers creamy/white).

Patterns are based on templates used for *Eucalyptus macrocarpa* — Rose of the West. For more realistic appearance, the flowers can have a curved template shape rather than one that's straight. Stem stitch in stamens.

Hakea laurina

Adapting blocks to depict other flora secies

Grevillea
This depicts a toothed-leaf species of the grevillea family. The leaves are the same as the dryandra. The flowers have stamens which are embroidered with stem stitch or couching.

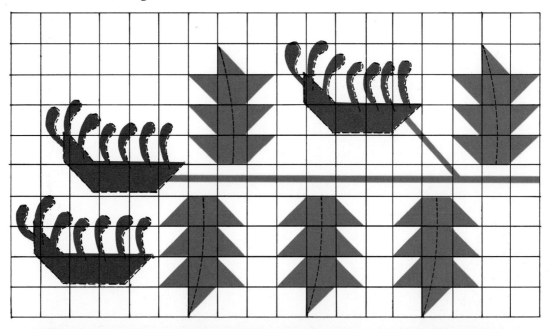

Grevillea species

These patterns depict the ziera family of plants, which closely resembles the boronia (it could also be used to depict the boronia).

The first pattern uses the same leaf formation as the wattle pattern 1, a 'log cabin' variation. The second pattern could be made by using the strip-piecing techniques to speed construction. The third uses the same flower units — small 'nine patch' squares along with the ½ square triangles for leaves. The aim of these patterns is to give an idea of the scale of these plants — they are very small flowers and when these blocks are sewn together you would get the 'mass flowered' effect of the plant.

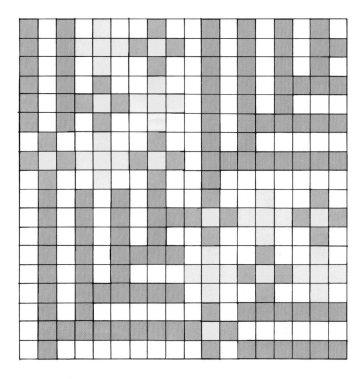

Pink Boronia

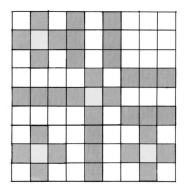

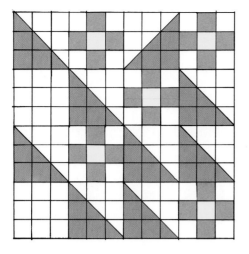

PINK BORONIA

This wall quilt depicts the pinnate leaf form of the
boronia. The 'feathery' leaf is captured using the
same corner start 'log cabin leaf' as used for some
of the wattle patterns.

CONSTRUCTION:
Machine pieced, hand quilted.

MEDIA:
Mixed cottons.

SIZE:
83 cm × 140 cm.

MAKER:
Sharon Blackie.

Patterns to depict native pea flowers

This pattern is for a realistic depiction which captures the character and proportions of pea flower plants.

The simplest way to depict these floral types would be to piece the flowers using the English or American piecing techniques, then to appliqué them to the pieced foundation of leaves. These flowers are quite small and are often grouped together along the stems. The orange-red pea flowers could depict the number of species commonly called 'eggs and bacon'. The yellow 'eye' would be best appliquéd in place before piecing. The mauve and purple pea flower depicts the hovea family. The red veins on the 'egg and bacon' and the purple veins on the hovea could be stem stitched.

Alternatively the flower may be presented in block form.

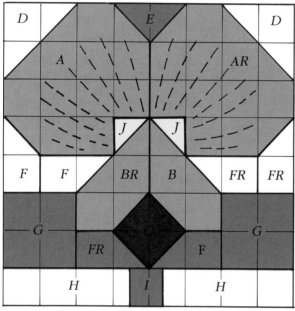

Hovea block

8 x 8 units

Pattern for hovea block in two sizes
30 cm (12 inch) and 20 cm (8 inch) on
pages 175 to 177.

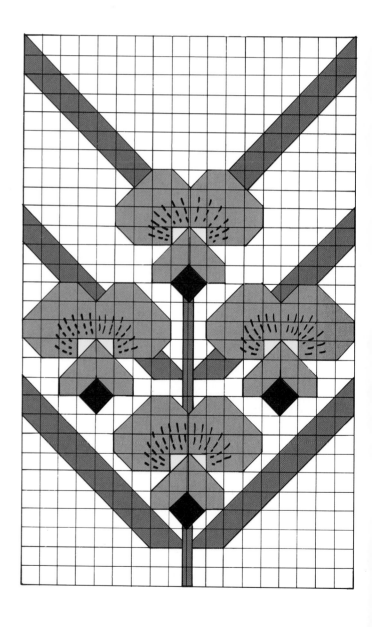

Dillwynia species

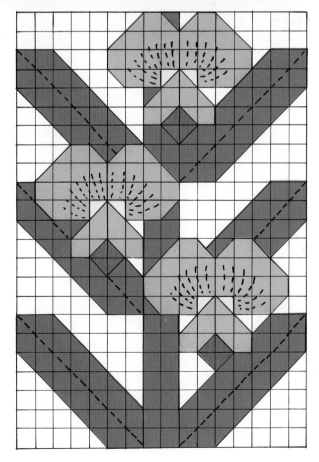

Patterns depict the native pea flowers. Use the relevant templates from the block pattern on pages 100 to 102 to piece flower motifs which could then be appliqued to a pieced foundation which could include the leaves. Alternatively the leaves could be also appliqued in place for this realistic depiction of the species.

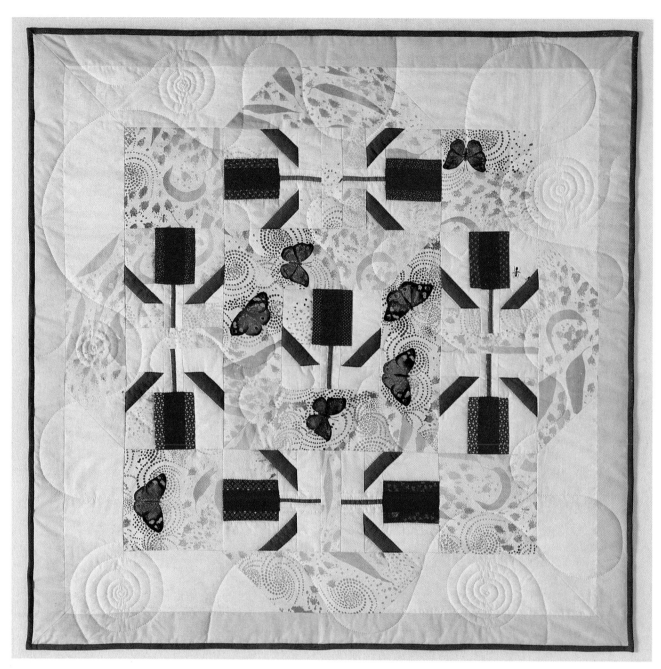

DANCE OF THE BROWNS

The bright red flowers and deep green foilage of the
callistemon contrast with the subtle screen printed
leaf patterns of the background and the warm
brown hues of the stencilled butterflies. Curved
lines of quilting suggest the flight of the butterflies
involved in a courting dance as they visit each flower
searching for nectar.

CONSTRUCTION:
Machine pieced, hand quilted. Hand printed and
stencilled background fabrics.

MEDIA:
Cotton prints, poplins, homespuns, calico.

SIZE:
85 cm × 85 cm.

MAKER:
Deborah Brearley

Using the Patterns in this Book

Frilled lizard

Using the full size patchwork templates

All the template patterns for the blocks are the exact size of the finished patch — they *do not* include a seam allowance.

The easiest way to use the templates from the book is to trace them using a sheet of template plastic (shiny side down), available from patchwork shops. Use a very sharp grey-lead pencil or better still a mechanical pencil which has a constant sharp point (HB leads), along with a ruler to maintain the straight edges. Use an old pair of fabric scissors to cut out the plastic templates accurately. These templates are now ready to use for the English papers method or American hand piecing techniques.

If you wish to have a seam allowance included in the template use a ¼ inch (6–7 mm) quilter's ruler to draw another line around the template pattern shapes drawn onto the plastic. Use this second line as the cutting line. Alternatively, rule up the second line the width of your choice if ¼ inch (6–7 mm) is not the desired size for a seam allowance.

You will notice that many of the template shapes are common to a number of the patterns, so check to see if you already have the shape made as a template before drafting and cutting out shapes for another block.

Checklist of patterns (page 41)
Before cutting out the fabric prepare a checklist of templates as in diagram 1. This will make the cutting out process simpler and speedier. Draw a small version of the template shape and note down how many are needed to make the block and which fabric is to be used.

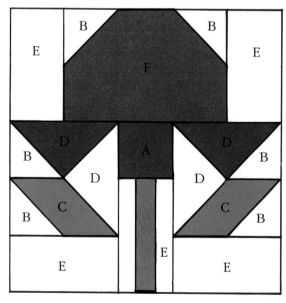

Waratah block

Pattern 1

A

Cut 1 — Flower bract

D

Cut 2 — Background
Cut 2 — Flower bracts

F

Cut 1 — Flower

B

Cut 6 — Background

E

Cut 5 — Background

C

Cut 2 — Leaves

Appliqué stem

Diagram 1   Checklist of templates for waratah block

*It is also a good idea to sketch a
diagram working out your piecing
sequence before piecing your block.*

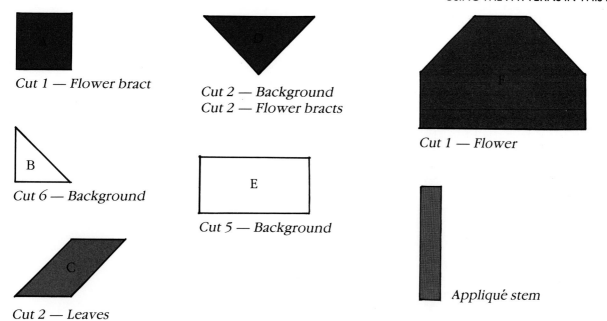

Diagram 2   Plan a piecing sequence for waratah block

Another method by which you can obtain very accurate template shapes is by the following process.

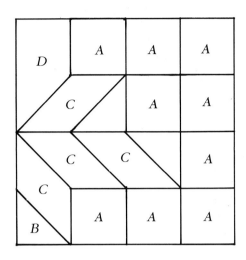

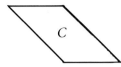

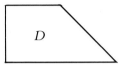

1. *Analyse the block and identify the template shapes, for example, wattle pattern uses the following shapes.*

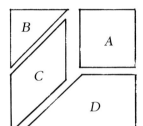
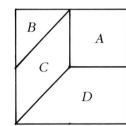

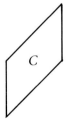
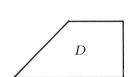

2. *See how these shapes may be interlocked (just like a jigsaw puzzle).*

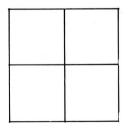

3. *Draw up a grid of the required size onto the template plastic or cardboard — this must be done accurately with a sharp pencil or mechanical pencil.*

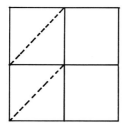

The four templates fit into a grid of 2 x 2 units.

4. *Pencil in additional diagonal lines required on the grid to outline template shapes (the dotted lines in the diagram).*

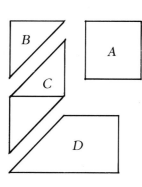

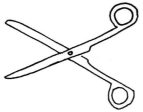

5. *Cut apart on appropriate lines for a set of very accurate templates (no seam allowance included). This is a very economical way of using your template plastic or cardboard.*

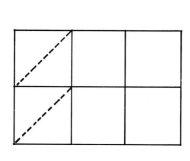

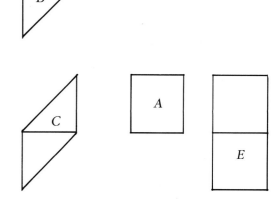

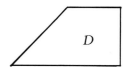

6. *Extend grid when more template shapes are required, for example 'E' template.*

Using the appliqué patterns

Appliqué patterns can be traced from the book in a similar fashion to the templates for piecing. Place template plastic or tracing paper over the master pattern and make a tracing of the required shape. This is a separate tracing and hence separate pattern for each colour or appropriate part of the bird or animal. Even if the wing and body are the same colour, trace the shapes off separately; the 'building up' of appliqué shapes can create a more realistic and 3-D appearance.

Using the appliqué patterns for quilting designs

If the fabric to be quilted is light in tone, then it can be placed directly over the master pattern which will be traced onto the fabric using a sharp grey-lead (HB) pencil or mechanical pencil (HB). If the fabric is dark-toned, then make a copy of the master pattern (trace it off onto a sheet of paper) and with a darning needle prick holes along all the lines. Take the pattern to a window, or better still, the glass or acrylic window of a light box.

Place the fabric or part of the quilt to be marked over the pattern. The light will shine through the needle holes allowing you to pencil HB or white-lead (good quality drawing pencil) in the quilting lines.

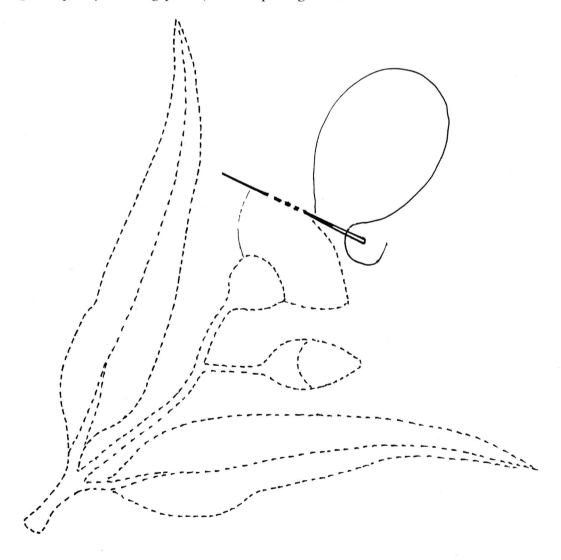

The Patchwork, Appliqué and Quilting Patterns

Emperor gum moth

Nine abstract blocks to explore

Block size 30 cm (12 inches)

Our red centre

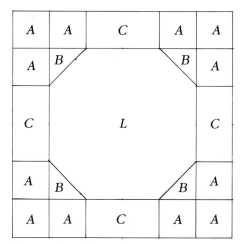

Our red centre

Heath

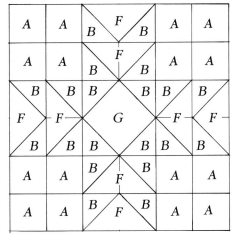

Heath

Sturt's desert pea

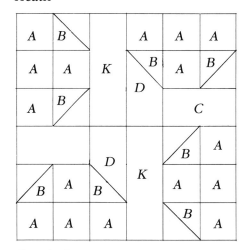

Sturt's desert pea

Templates placement indicated needed for each block

Nine abstract blocks to explore (continued)

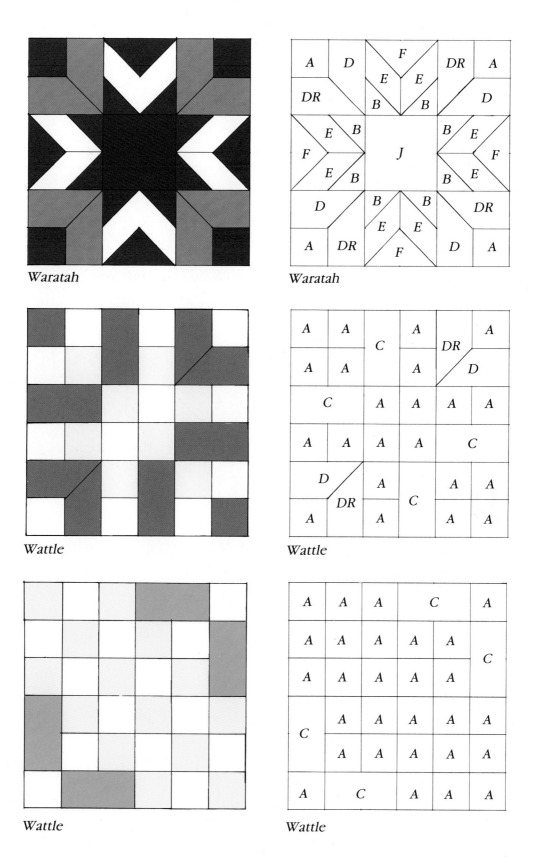

Waratah

Waratah

Wattle

Wattle

Wattle

Wattle

Nine abstract blocks to explore (continued)

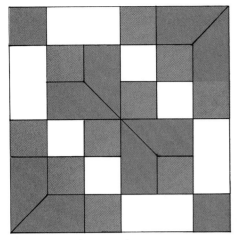

Mint bush/hovea/westringia

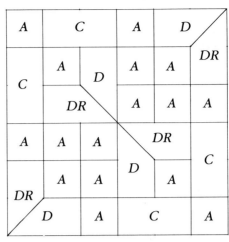

Mint bush/hovea/westringia

Galahs in flight

Banksia

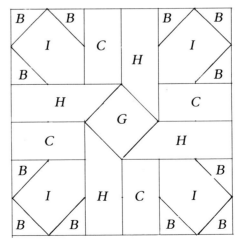

Banksia

Templates for 'Nine abstract blocks to explore'

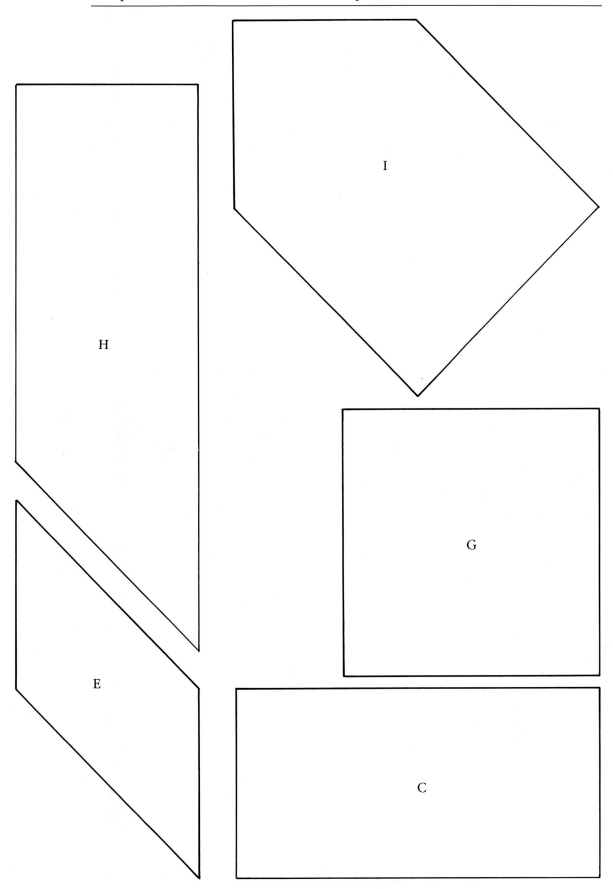

Templates for 'Nine abstract blocks to explore' (continued)

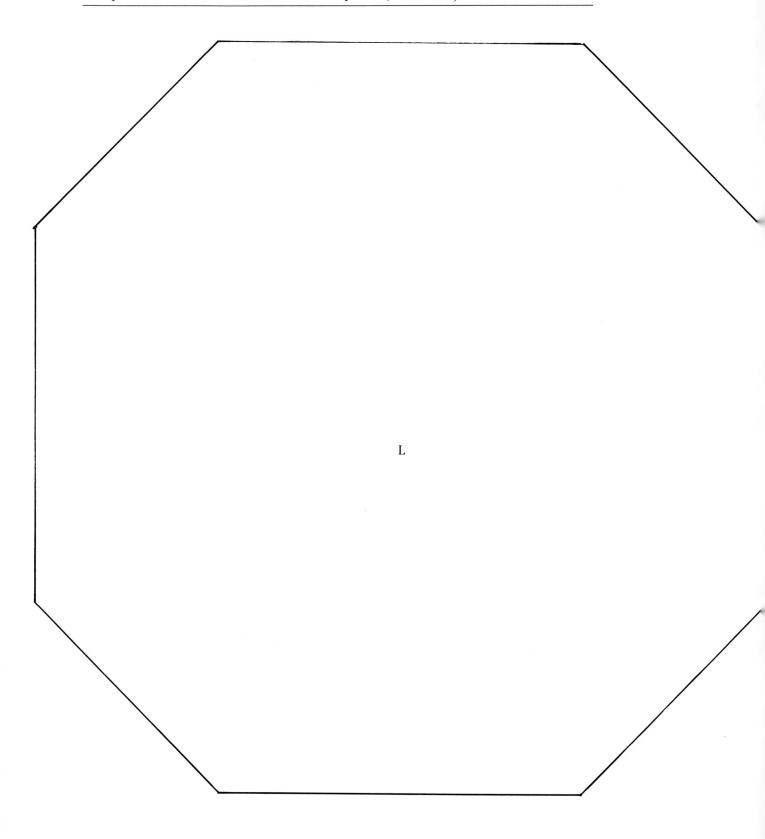

L

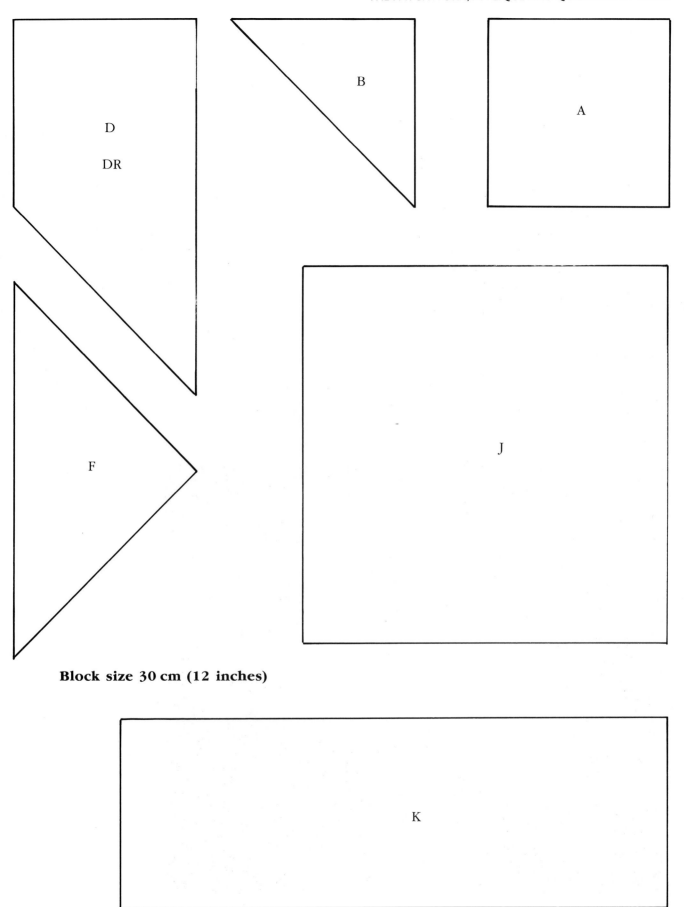

Block size 30 cm (12 inches)

Wattle

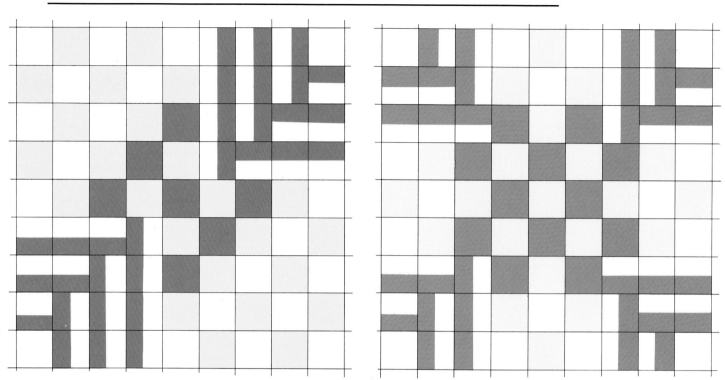

Wattle pattern 1

Wattle pattern 2

Wattle species

Wattle templates for blocks 1 and 2

The 'B' Template indicates the finished width of the leaf and background pieces. It is to be used as a strip cutting template (add the desired seam allowance). The length of the template is optional — often determined by the width of the fabric being used. The length of the fabric strips is optional as the strips are trimmed as the construction of the leaf unit takes place. The leaf unit is constructed along the lines of a corner start log cabin sequence.

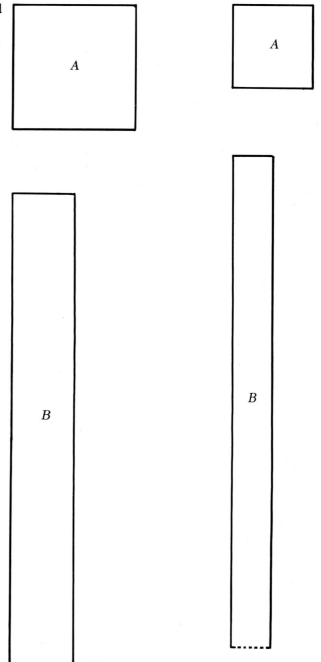

Templates do not include a seam allowance

Block size 20 cm (8 inches)

Block size 30 cm (12 inches)

Broken line, extend length of template to desired size

A   Wattle blossom and background
B   Leaf shape and background

Using part of wattle pattern 1 (a corner consisting of 6 x 6 units) to make the blocks for a quilt. Sixteen blocks are needed to make up this quilt.

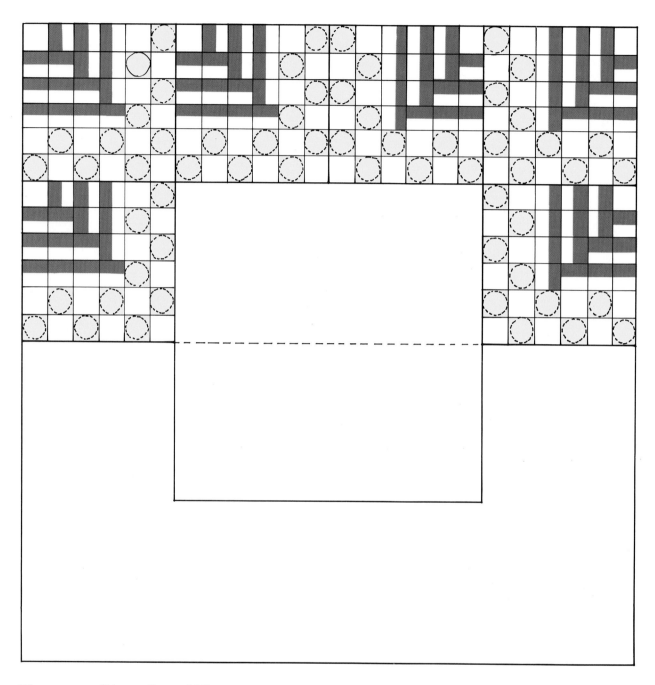

The centre of the quilt could feature appliquéd birds or animals or it could be quilted with wattle sprays or an echo of the block pattern.

This pattern could be the centre medallion for a much larger quilt also . . . the possibilities are endless.

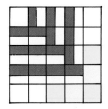

This block is a corner of pattern 1, wattle, made up of 5 x 5 units. The pattern for this quilt is made up of an arrangement of 20 blocks.

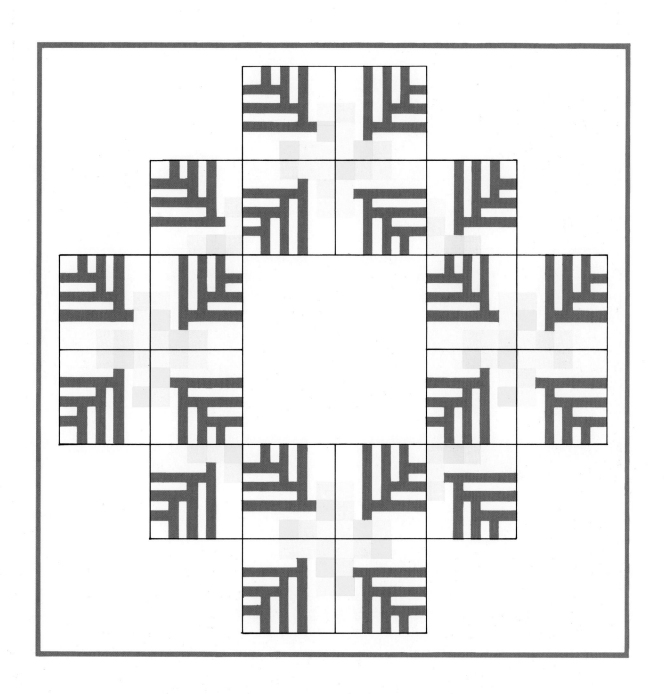

WATTLE POOL

The quilt is the development of a basic wattle block. The arrangement of colour and shapes suggests the blossom and leaves of the wattle fallen into a pool of water which is reflecting the blue of the sky. The wind has blown the blossom to the outer edges of the pool. Circles of quilting suggest the movement of the water as another blossom drops into the blue pool.

MEDIA:
Cotton prints and plains.
SIZE:
154 cm × 154 cm.
MAKER:
Deborah Brearley.

This quilt illustrates the patterns on pages 52 to 55.

Wattle patterns 2 and 3

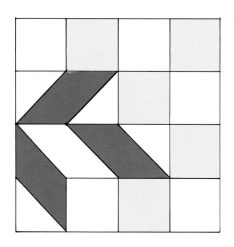 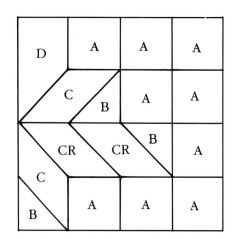

Block size 20 cm (8 inches)

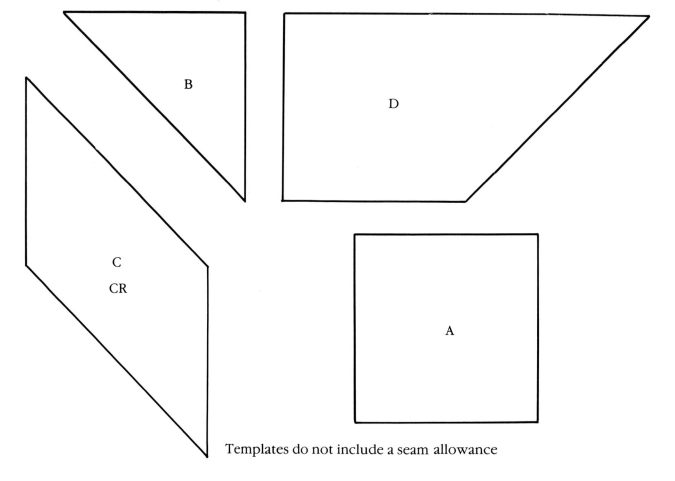

Templates do not include a seam allowance

Block size 30 cm (12 inches)

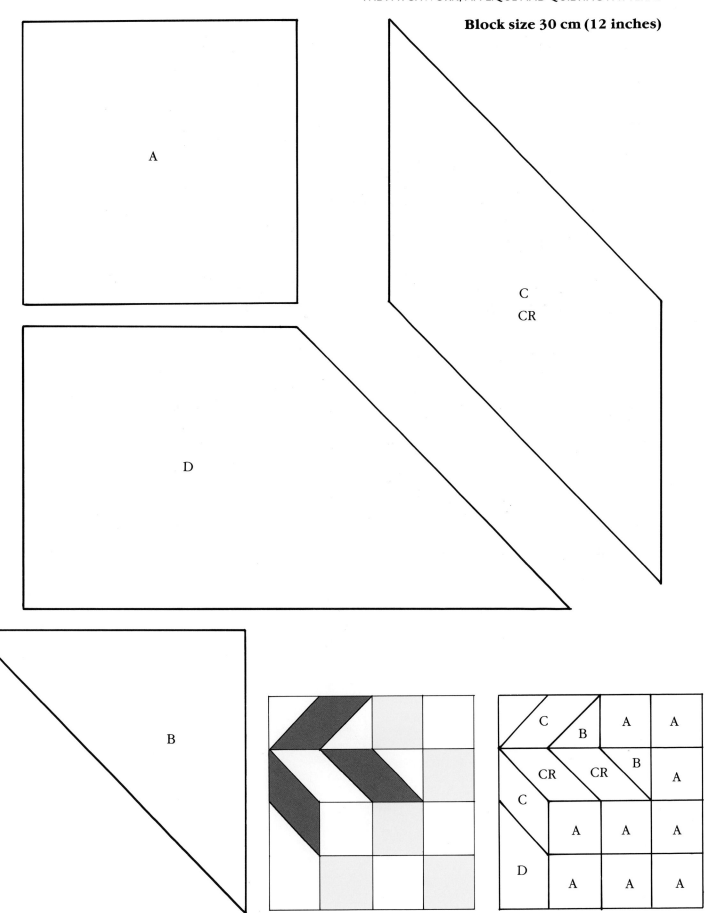

This block is pattern 2 with an additional row of squares to extend the wattle blossoms so forming a rectangular block which increases the number of design possibilities from the basic block.

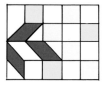 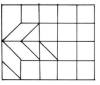

5 x 4 units   Template placement

Make 12 blocks of main block 5 x 4 units and 4 'adapted' blocks of leaf units to complete quilt arrangement. The outlined shapes indicate how the blocks are laid out for this quilt design. Count up the number of units in the outlined 'filler' rectangles to determine their size to complete quilt.

Leaf unit for centre of quilt — less joins can be made if you wish by using rectangular templates instead of squares in the appropriate places.

Fairy wren

The fairy wrens *(Genus malurus)* are among the best known of our small birds, 14 to 15 cm including tail. Their colour varies, blues with browns, black, red depending on the species and sex, but their long tails held vertically make them easy to recognise. They are nearly always seen in family groups, flitting about together feeding and chatting with a musical trill. A family group is a joy to watch; they are quite bold and will flit around you continuously if you are in their territory.

FAIRY WRENS

The pair of fairy wrens have been depicted using the shadow applique technique. A number of coloured fabrics have been placed under a fine chiffon and then the birds and details have been outlined with quilting and embroidery stitches.

MEDIA:
cottons, polyester chiffon.
SIZE:
55 cm × 55 cm.
MAKER:
Deborah Brearley.

Fairy wrens

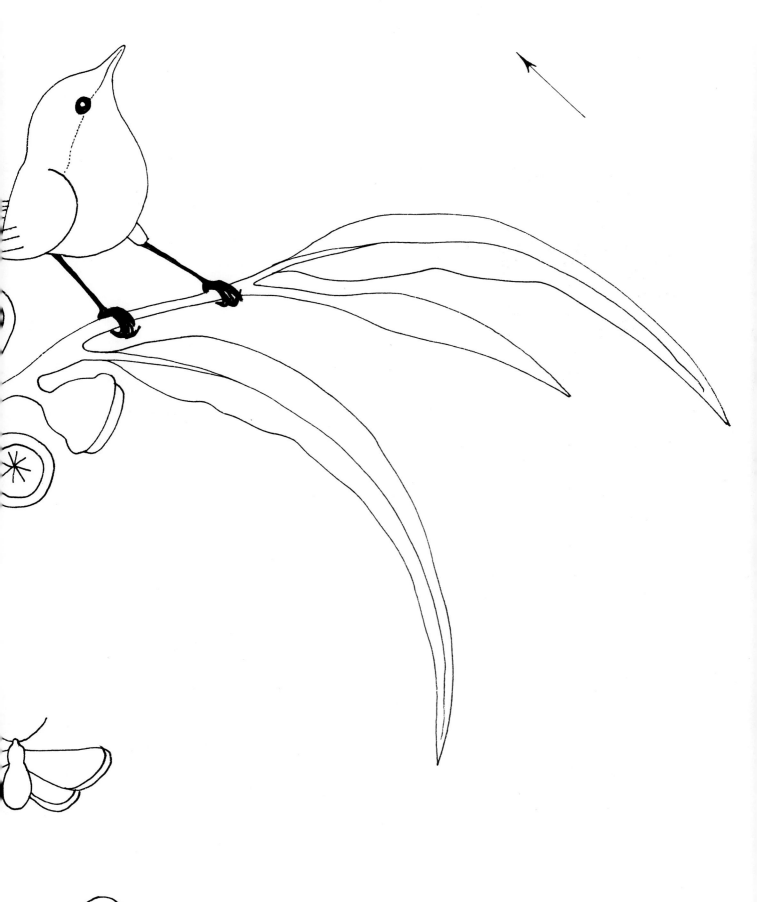

Waratah

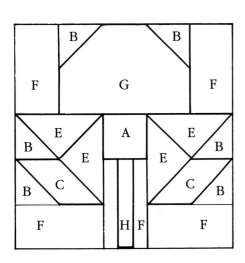

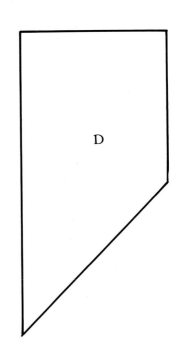

Block size 20 cm (8 inches)

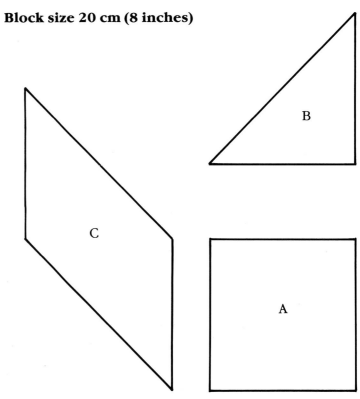

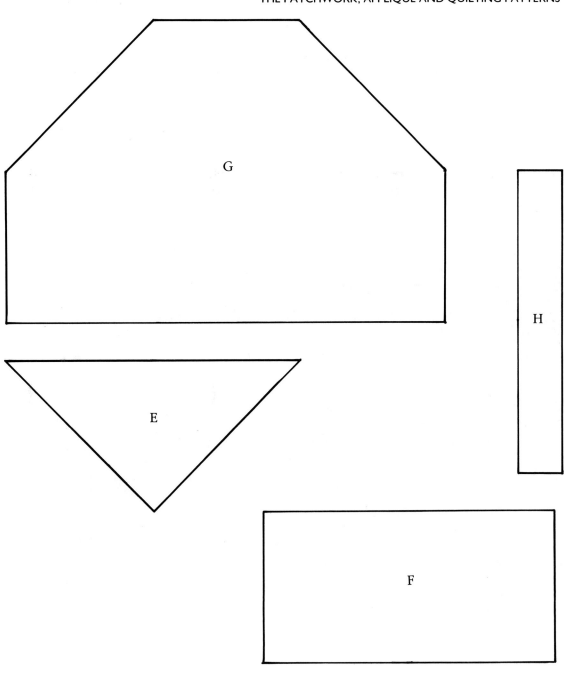

Alternative block division where template 'D' has been included.

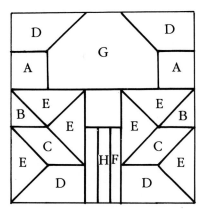

Waratah

Block size 30 cm (12 inches)

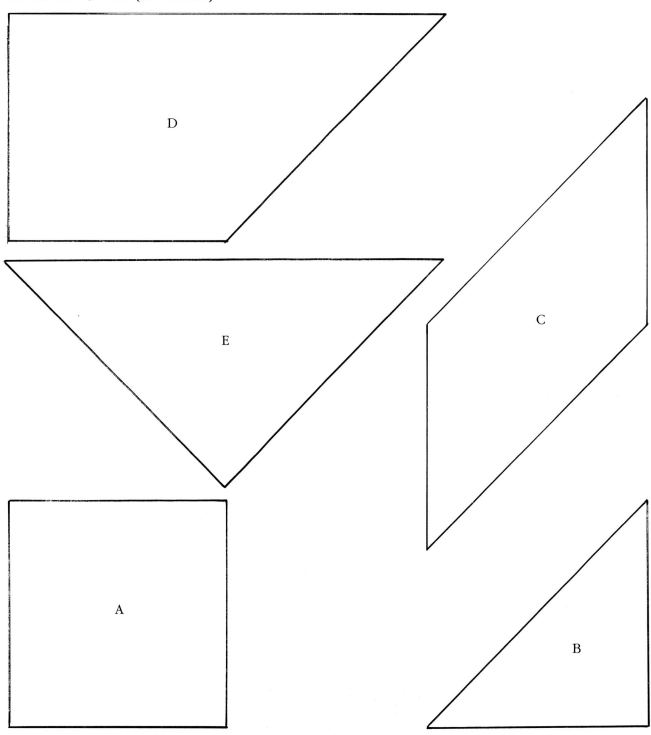

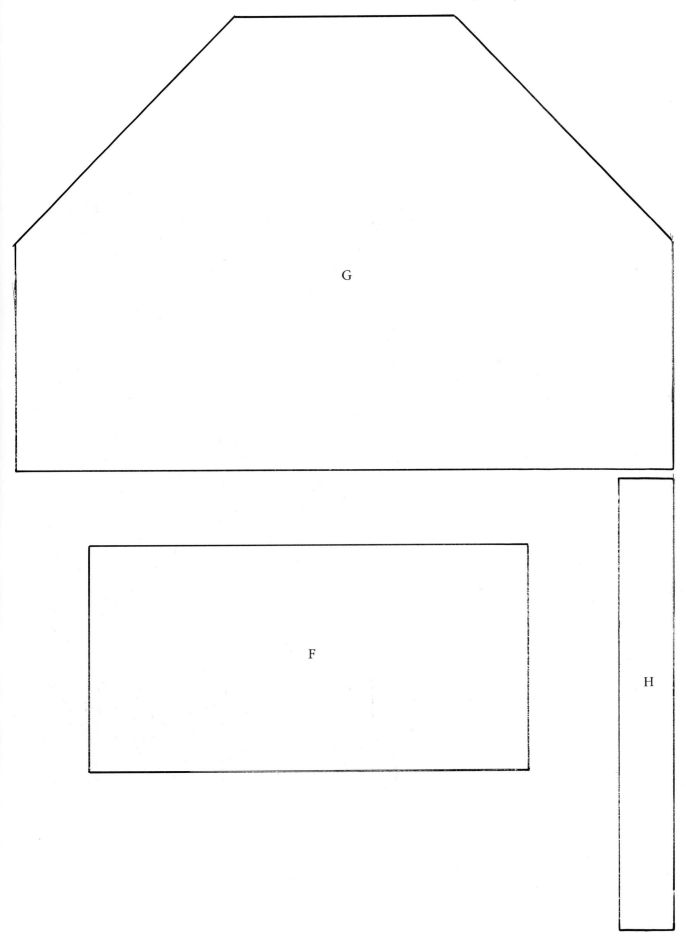

G

F

H

Banksia

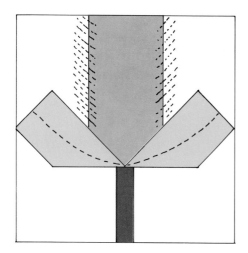

Pattern 1

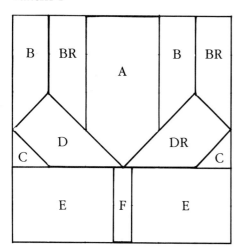

Banksia quilt
46 x 34 units

Banksia pattern 1

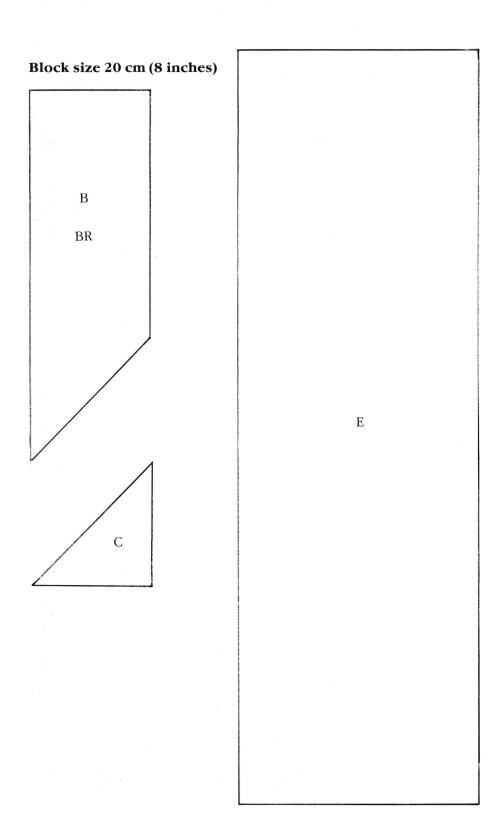

Block size 20 cm (8 inches)

B

BR

C

E

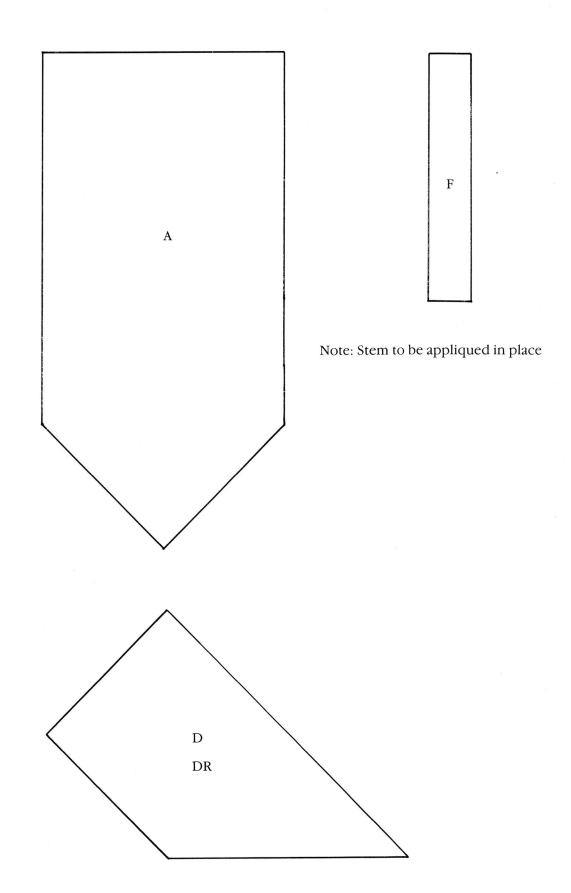

A

F

Note: Stem to be appliqued in place

D
DR

Banksia pattern 1 (continued)

Block size 30 cm (12 inches)

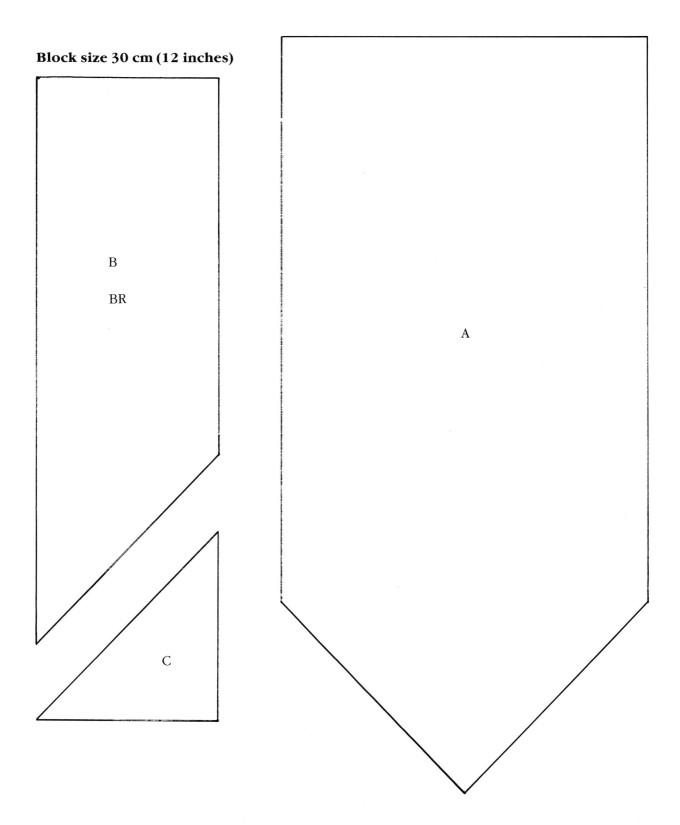

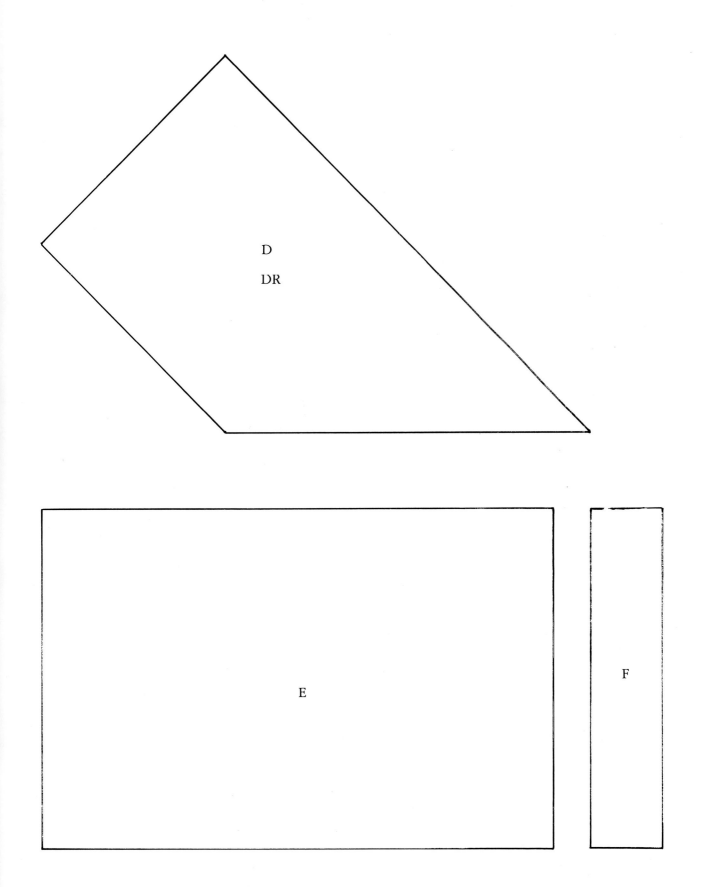

Banksia pattern 2

Block size 20 cm (8 inches)

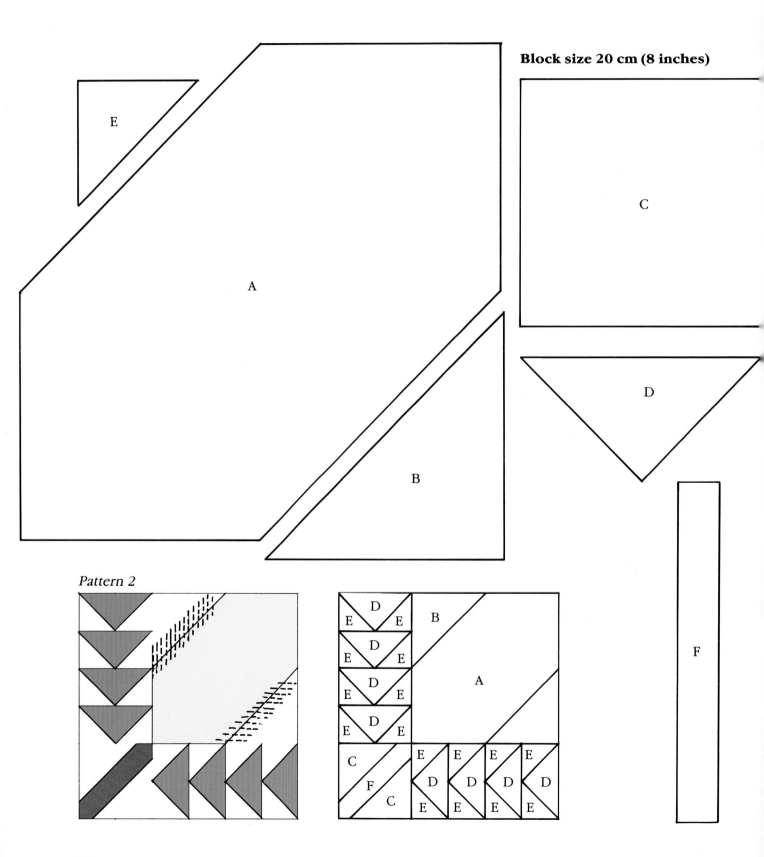

Pattern 2

Banksia and yellow tailed black cockatoo quilt

This quilt would be an effective medallion as part of a much larger quilt.

28 x 28 units

If you wish to make the banksia and yellow tailed black cockatoo quilt use a 20 cm (8 inch) block. This will ensure that the flowers in proportion to the cockatoo are the same as illustrated in this diagram.

Banksia pattern 2 (continued)

Block size 30 cm (12 inches)

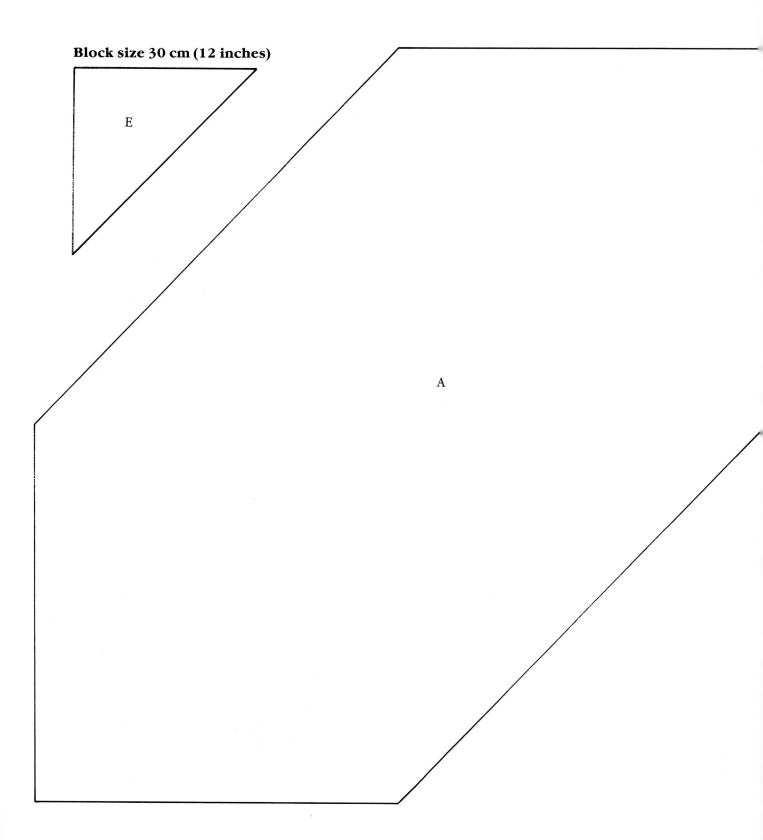

E

A

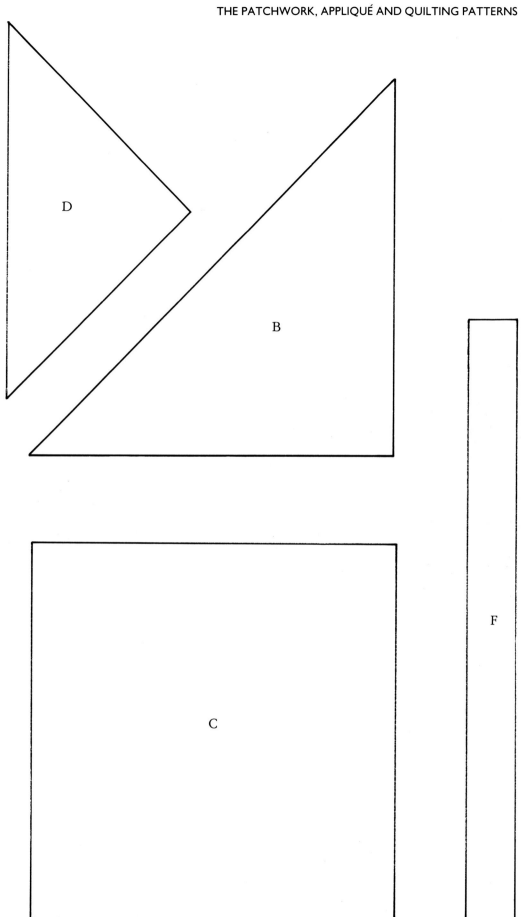

Yellow tailed black cockatoo

78

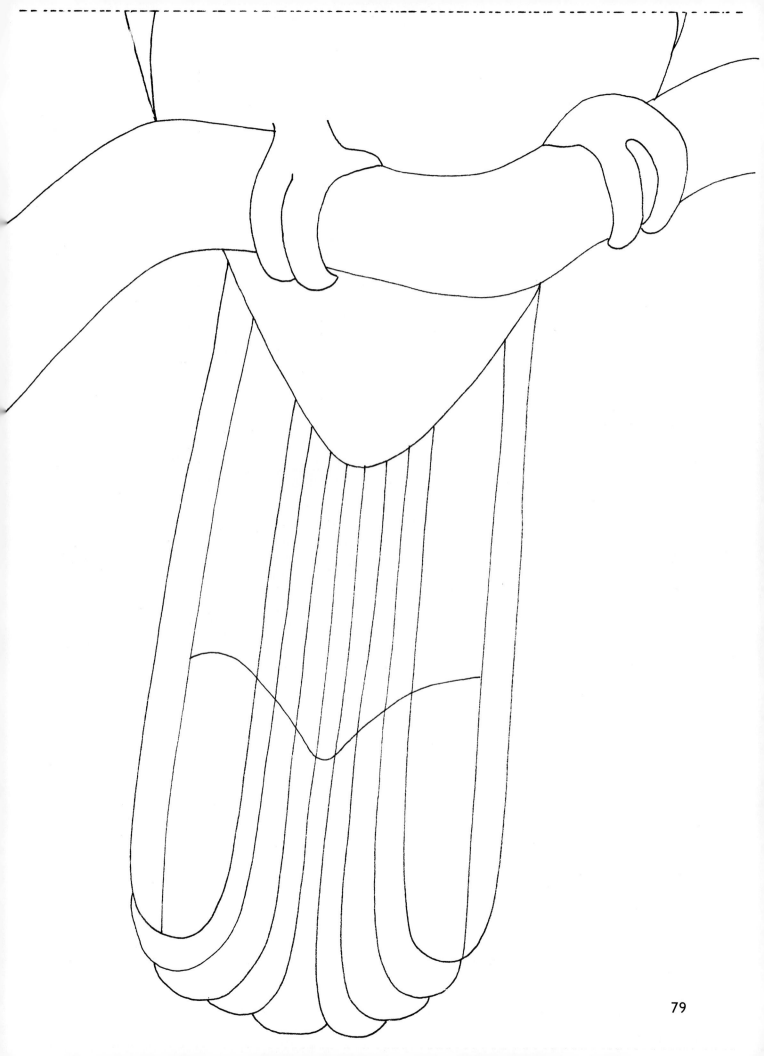

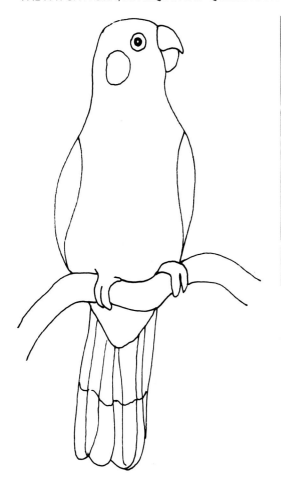

Yellow tailed black cockatoo

BANKSIAS AND YELLOW TAILED BLACK COCKATOO

The yellow tailed black cockatoo is one of the
largest cockatoos measuring 56 – 66 cm in length.
One of its favourite foods is the seeds of the
banksia.

CONSTRUCTION:
Hand pieced and quilted.

MEDIA:
Printed and plain cottons.

SIZE:
88 cm × 92 cm.

MAKER:
Jenny Agnew.

Banksia pattern 3

Block size 20 cm (8 inches)

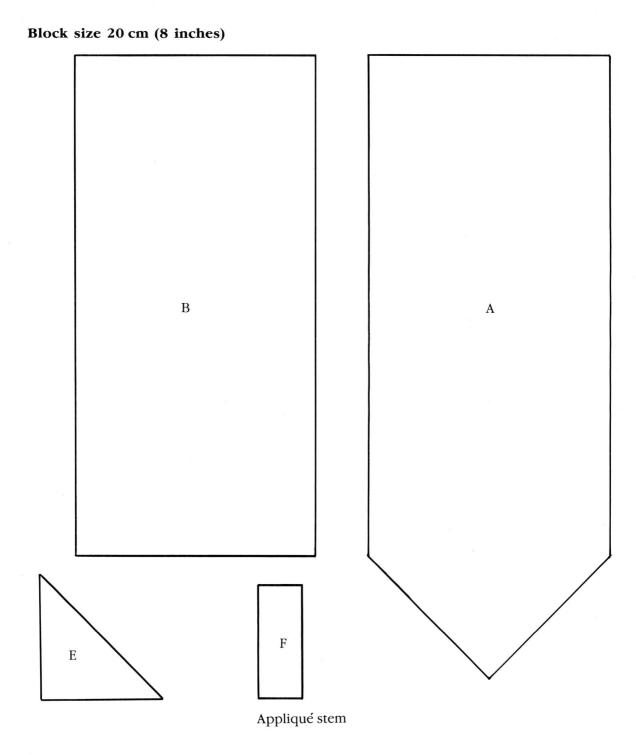

Appliqué stem

Templates for block

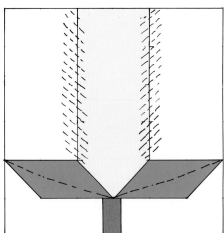

Pattern 3

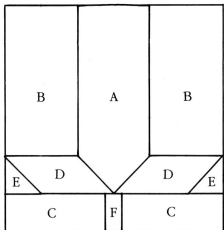

Banksia integrifolia (coastal banksia)

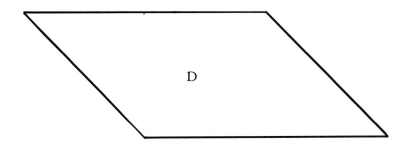

Banksia pattern 3 (continued)

Block size 30 cm (12 inches)

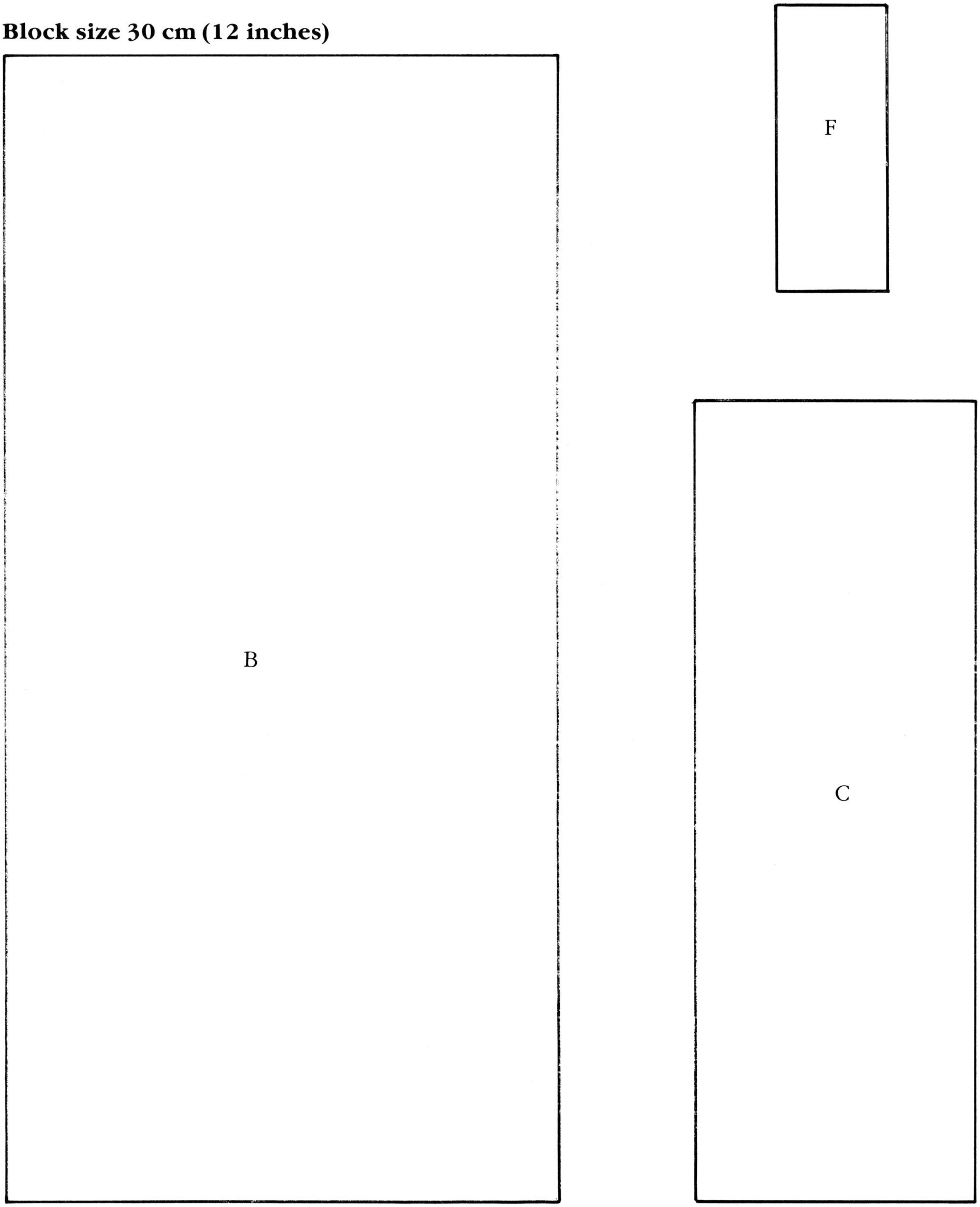

B

F

C

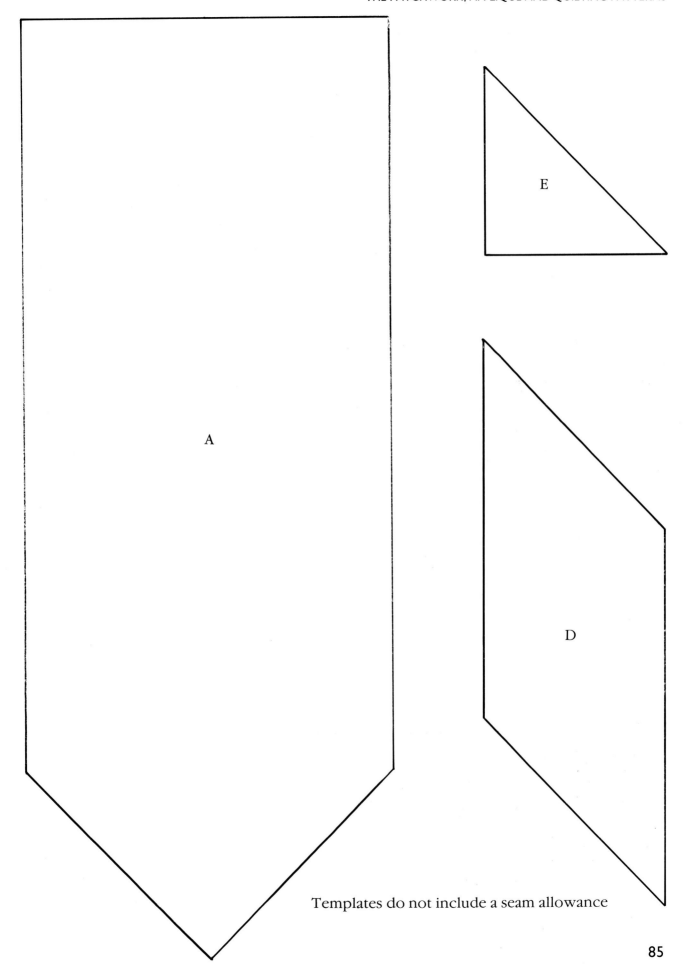

E

A

D

Templates do not include a seam allowance

Dryandra

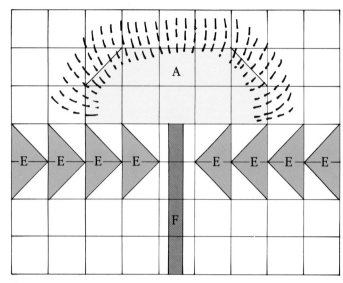

Pattern 1

Dryandra

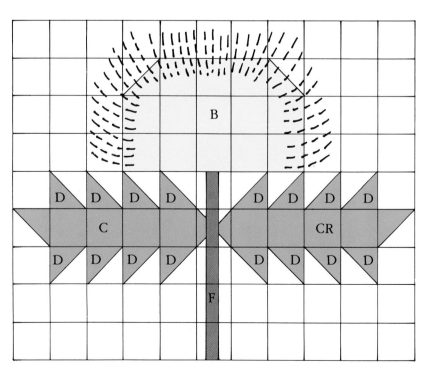

Pattern 2

Templates for both blocks

Block size 20 cm (8 inches)

A   Flower head pattern no. 1
B   Flower head pattern no. 2
C   Centre of leaf pattern no. 2
D   Leaf serrations pattern no. 2
E   Leaf segment pattern no. 1
F   Stem patterns nos. 1 & 2

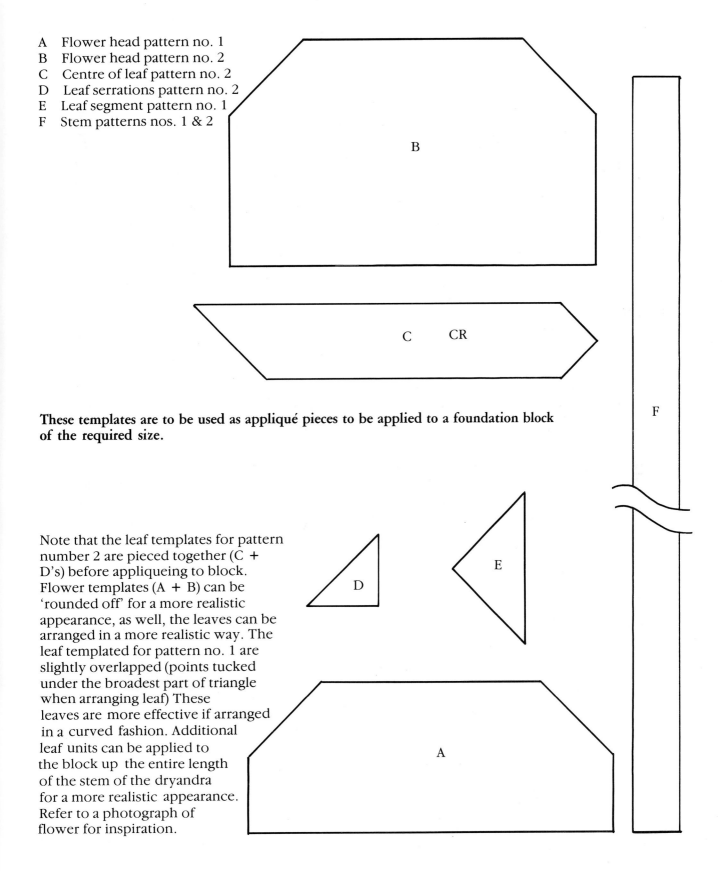

These templates are to be used as appliqué pieces to be applied to a foundation block of the required size.

Note that the leaf templates for pattern number 2 are pieced together (C + D's) before appliqueing to block. Flower templates (A + B) can be 'rounded off' for a more realistic appearance, as well, the leaves can be arranged in a more realistic way. The leaf templated for pattern no. 1 are slightly overlapped (points tucked under the broadest part of triangle when arranging leaf) These leaves are more effective if arranged in a curved fashion. Additional leaf units can be applied to the block up the entire length of the stem of the dryandra for a more realistic appearance. Refer to a photograph of flower for inspiration.

Callistemon

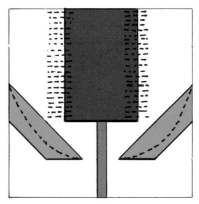

Pattern 1

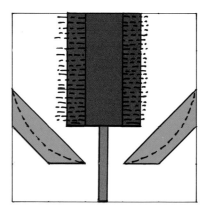

Pattern 2

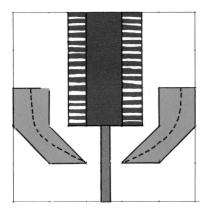

Pattern 3

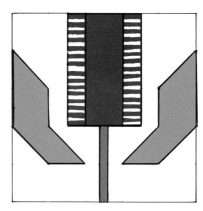

Pattern 4

CALLISTEMON

A repeat of a callistemon block to make this
delightful miniature quilt.

MEDIA:
Cotton prints and plains.

SIZE:
59 cm × 46 cm.

MAKER:
Lesley Duffy.

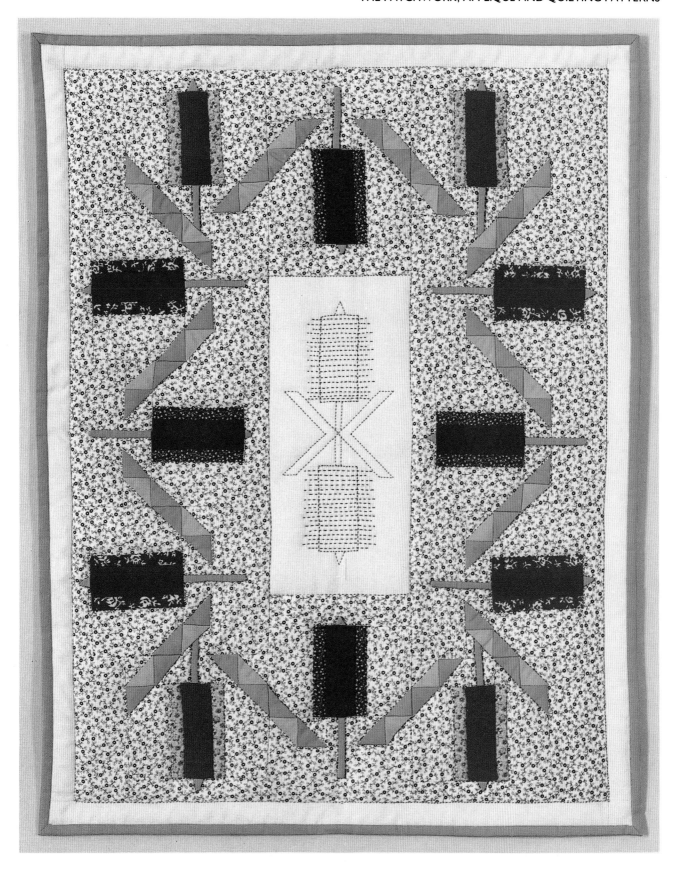

Callistemon patterns 1, 2, 3 & 4

Block size 20 cm (8 inches)

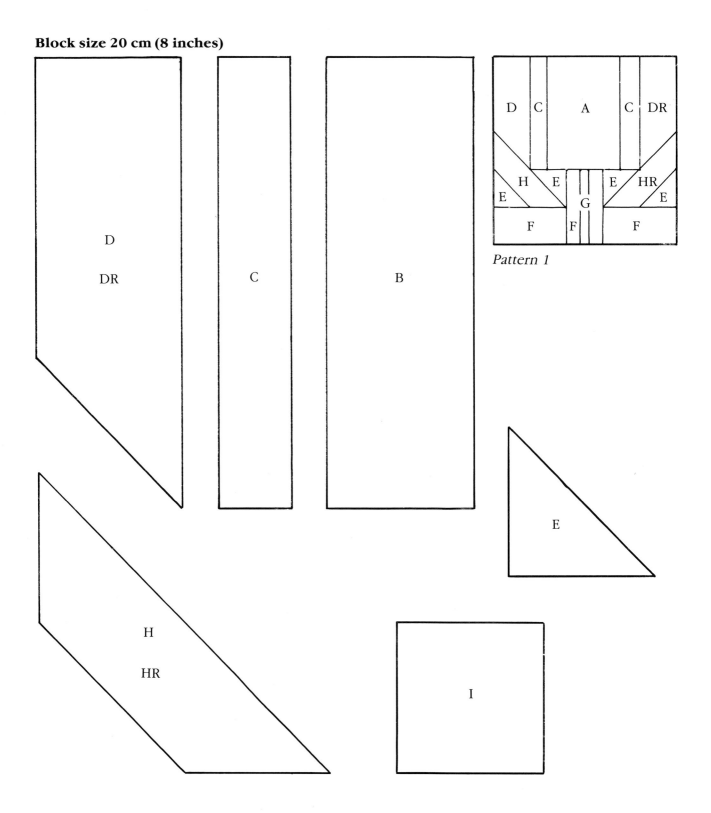

Pattern 1

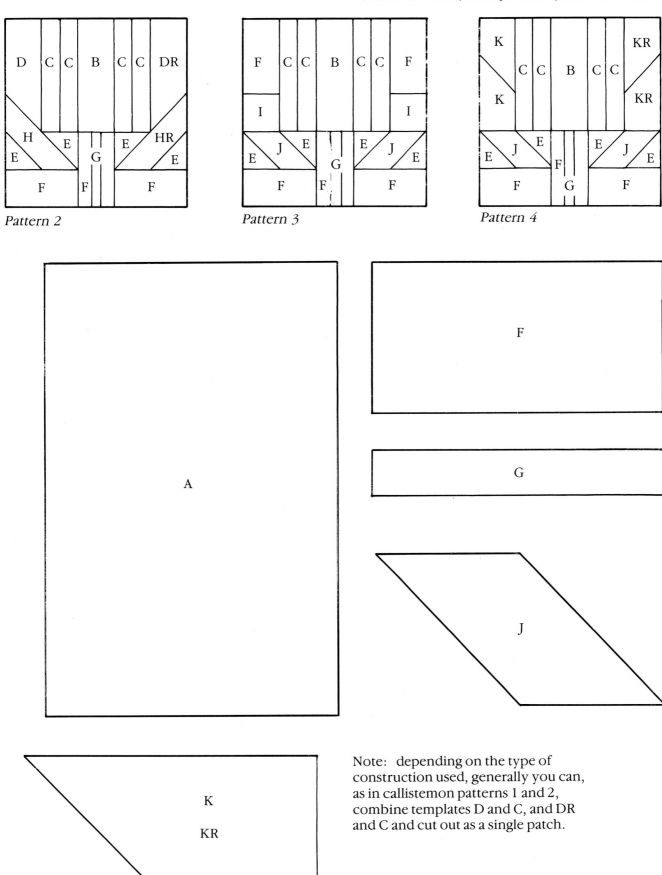

Pattern 2

Pattern 3

Pattern 4

Note: depending on the type of construction used, generally you can, as in callistemon patterns 1 and 2, combine templates D and C, and DR and C and cut out as a single patch.

Callistemon patterns 1, 2, 3 & 4 (continued)

Block size 30 cm (12 inches)

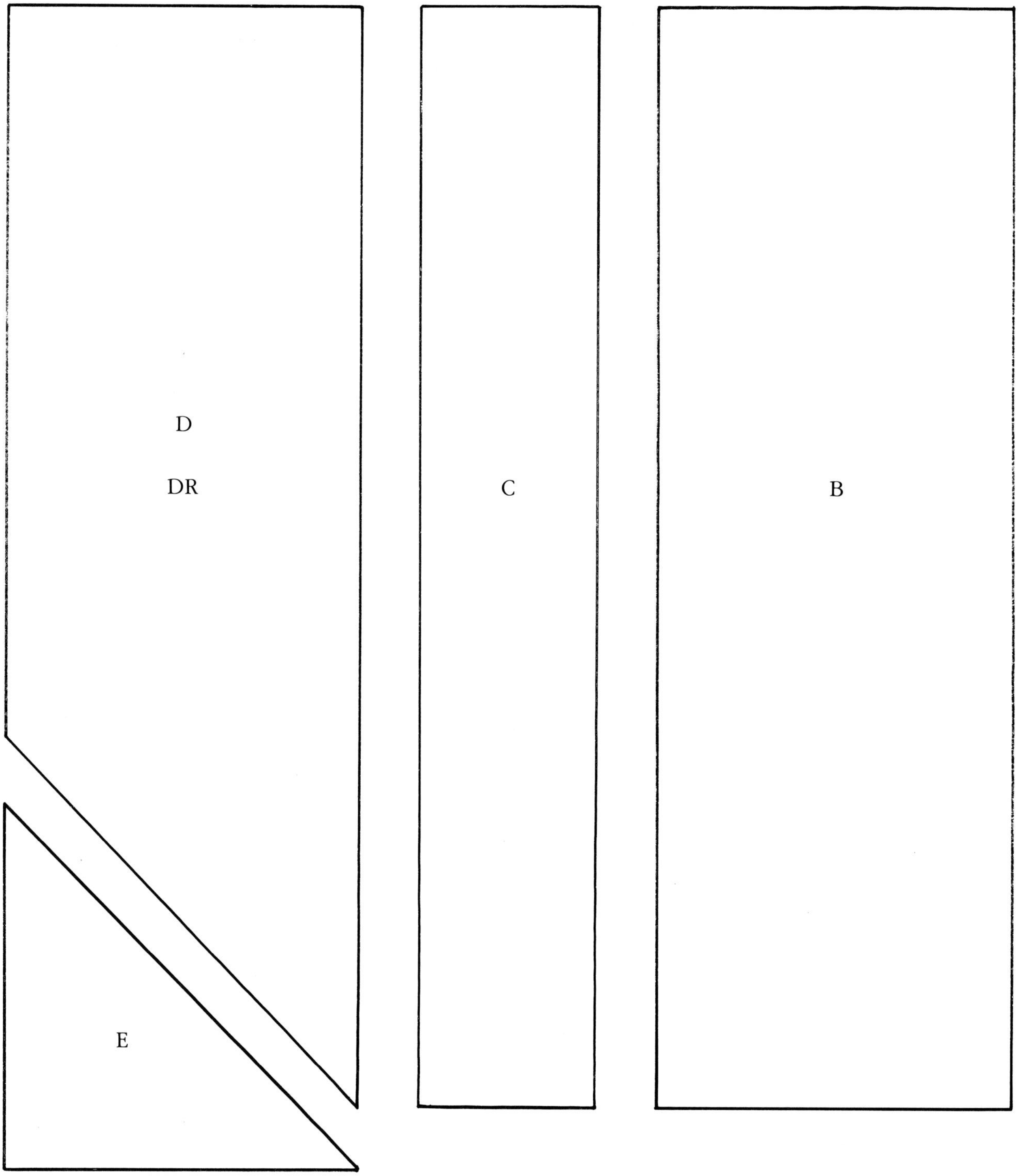

D

DR

C

B

E

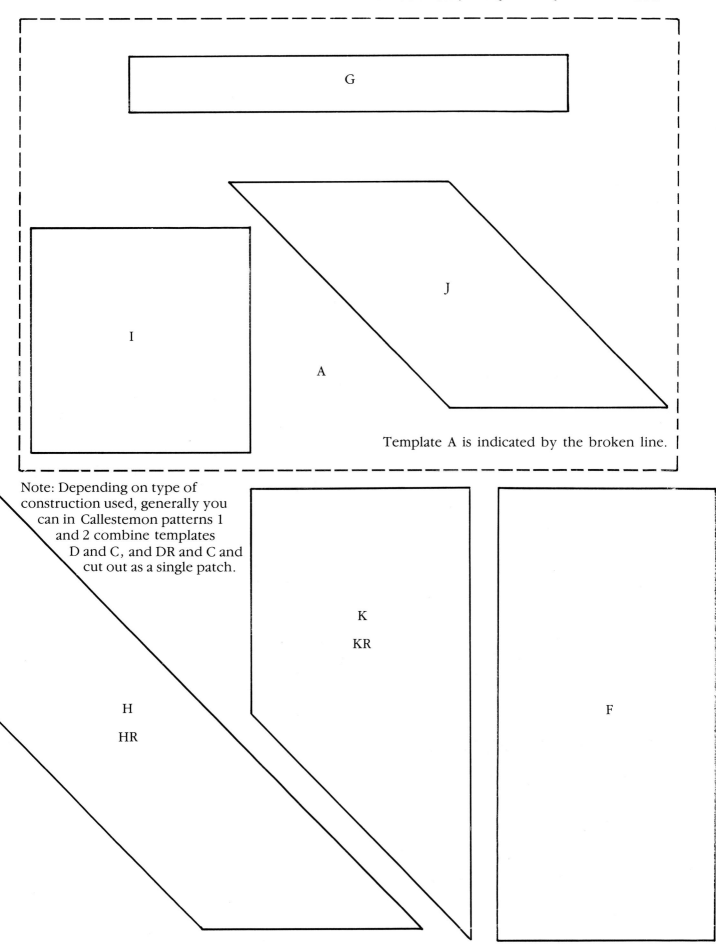

G

I

J

A

Template A is indicated by the broken line.

Note: Depending on type of construction used, generally you can in Callestemon patterns 1 and 2 combine templates D and C, and DR and C and cut out as a single patch.

H
HR

K
KR

F

These diagrams illustrate two quilts which could be constructed using callistemon blocks. These quilts were designed using the 'colour, cut and paste' technique outlined in 'Exploring the Patterns', page 10. The size of the quilt will depend on the size of the unit chosen to draw up templates or on the block size chosen (templates for the callistemon pattern block appear on pages 90 and 92 in two sizes: 30cm (12 inch) and 20 cm (8 inch)).

Callistemon and butterfly quilt

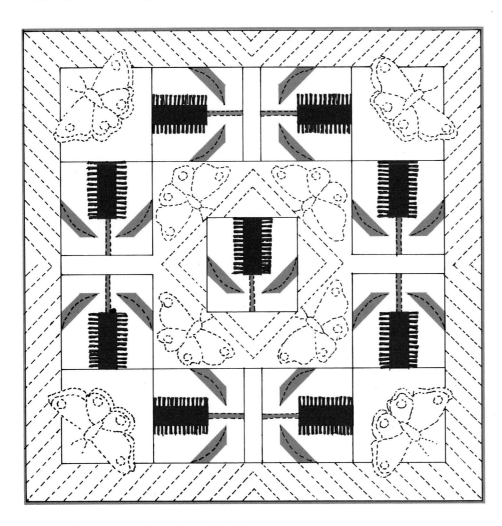

This quilt design is based on 25 x 25 units.

Callistemon and butterfly quilt

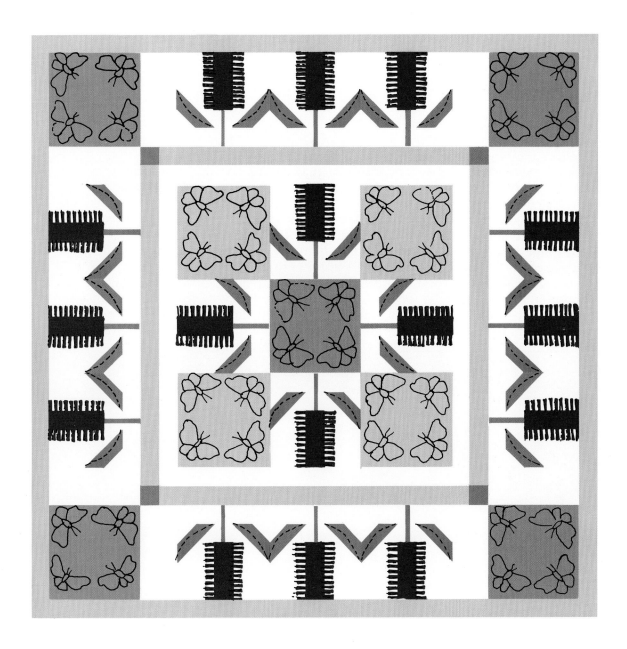

This quilt design is based on 31 x 31
units.

Butterflies and moths

The butterfly and moth patterns are depicted larger than life, so that they appear close to scale when used along with the flora patterns.

They are intended to be used primarily as quilting patterns, the lines suggesting their decorative markings. Consider using them for embroidery, appliqué or even stencil patterns.

The common brown (*Heteronympha merope*) and the wanderer (*Danaus plexippus*) are species seen throughout most of the country.

The emperor gum moth (*Antheraea eucalypti*) is probably better known in its larva stage. These enormous caterpillars are a very colourful blue-green with a pale lateral stripe and red and blue tufts of spines along the back and sides. Many of these fellows are kept as 'pets'. Keeping them in a shoe box, feeding them continually, you were usually rewarded with a display of cocoon building. Then much later, there emerged a beautiful moth with a wingspan up to 13 cm across, with colourful 'eyes' on its wings, a 'hairy' body and feathery antennae.

Wanderer

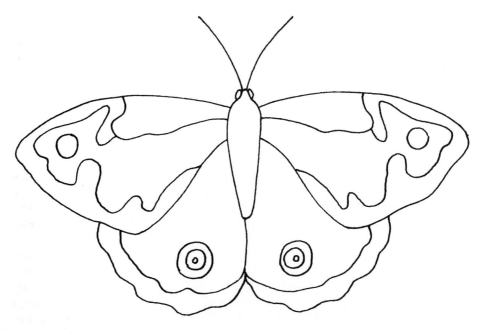

Common brown

Swordgrass brown

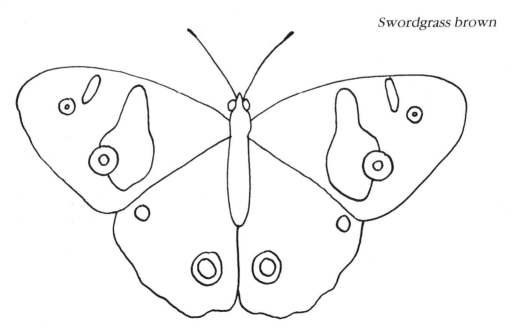

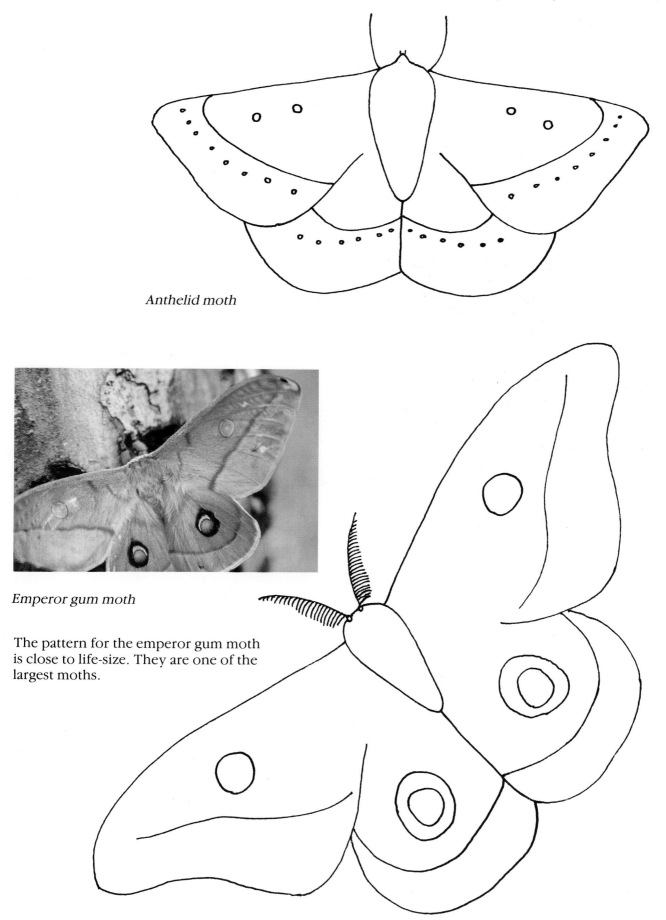

Anthelid moth

Emperor gum moth

The pattern for the emperor gum moth is close to life-size. They are one of the largest moths.

Sturt's desert pea pattern 1

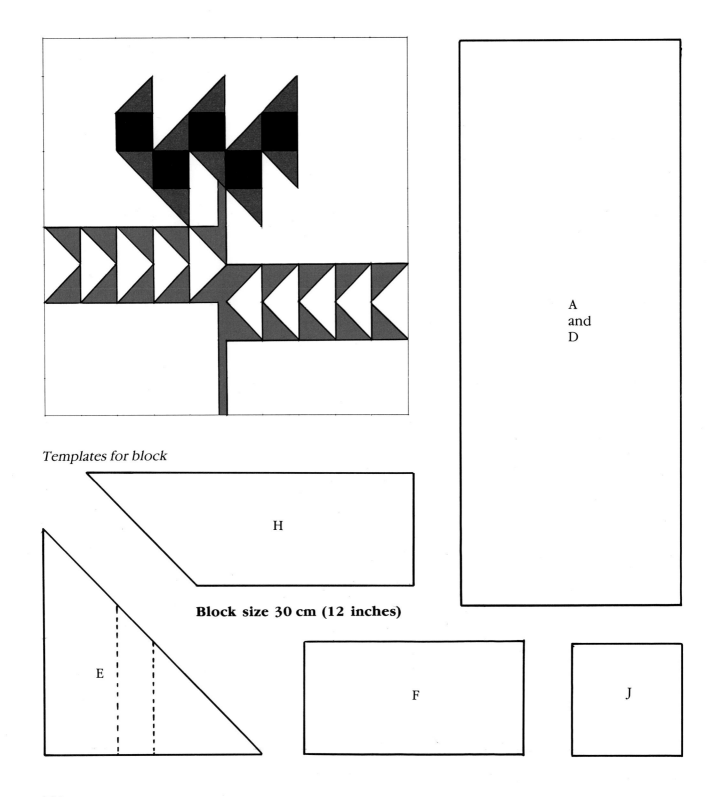

Templates for block

Block size 30 cm (12 inches)

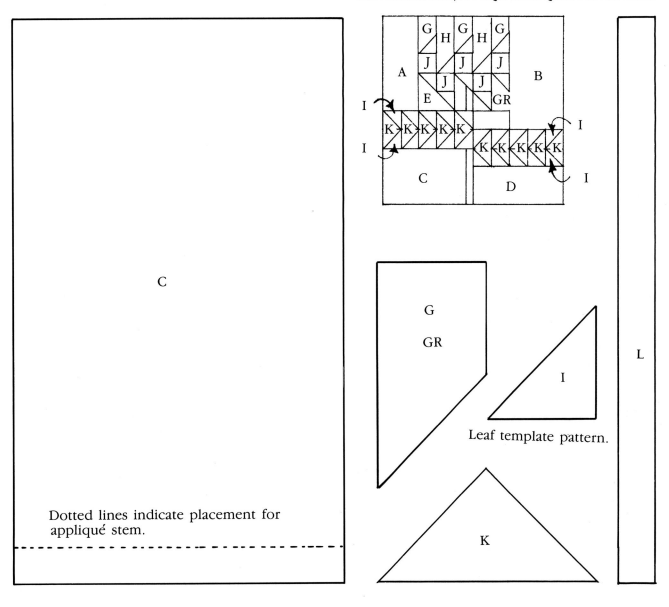

C

Dotted lines indicate placement for appliqué stem.

G
GR

I

Leaf template pattern.

K

L

B

Sturt's desert pea pattern 2

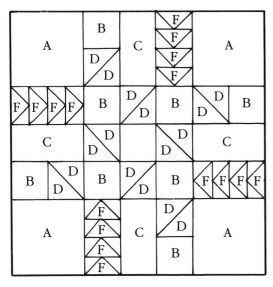

Block size 49 cm

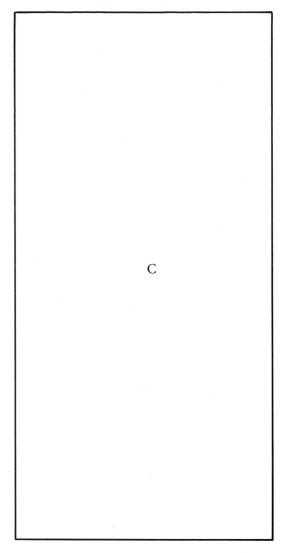

C

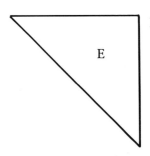

Leaf template pattern.

E

This block has been presented in a larger size so that the leaf and background patterns (E and F) are of a reasonable size for easy piecing.

Templates for full size block

STURT'S DESERT PEA QUILT

This quilt illustrates the repetition of a basic block pattern. The units of the blocks have been overlapped, that is, the leaf units 'invade' the grid units on the adjoining blocks, so that the overall quilt design is more compact. The leaf template has also been used to make a traditional saw-tooth border. Black taffeta has been used to suggest the shiny black boss of the flower.

MEDIA:
Cottons, poly-cottons, taffeta.

SIZE:
160 cm × 104 cm.

MAKER:
Margaret Davey.

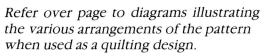

The Sturt's desert pea motifs could be used for a pieced quilt background for a number of quilted bearded dragons.

Refer over page to diagrams illustrating the various arrangements of the pattern when used as a quilting design.

Bearded dragon

One of the reptile family in Australia, the bearded dragon (*Amphibolurus barbatus*) is one of the most widespread of lizards. It is 25 cm or more in length and it sports a bearded throat. It varies in colour from light grey to dark brown depending on its environment. When frightened, it will adopt a ferocious open-mouthed stance displaying its golden yellow mouth and tongue and its spiny beard. If pressed, it can run on its back legs.

This pattern is intended primarily as a quilting design; it could be used as an appliqué design — by machine. The tiny claws and spikes would prove to be a hand appliqué nightmare! Consider embroidering the design as part of a quilt.

Bearded dragon *A. barbatus*

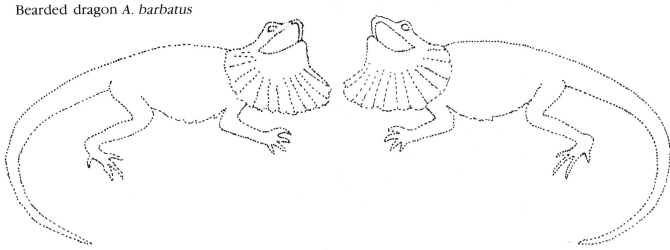

The dragons could be placed like this
to border a quilt.

The dragons could be placed head-to-tail fashion down the quilt, alternating with pieced desert pea (or other flower) motifs.

Bearded dragon

Eucalyptus blossom pattern 1

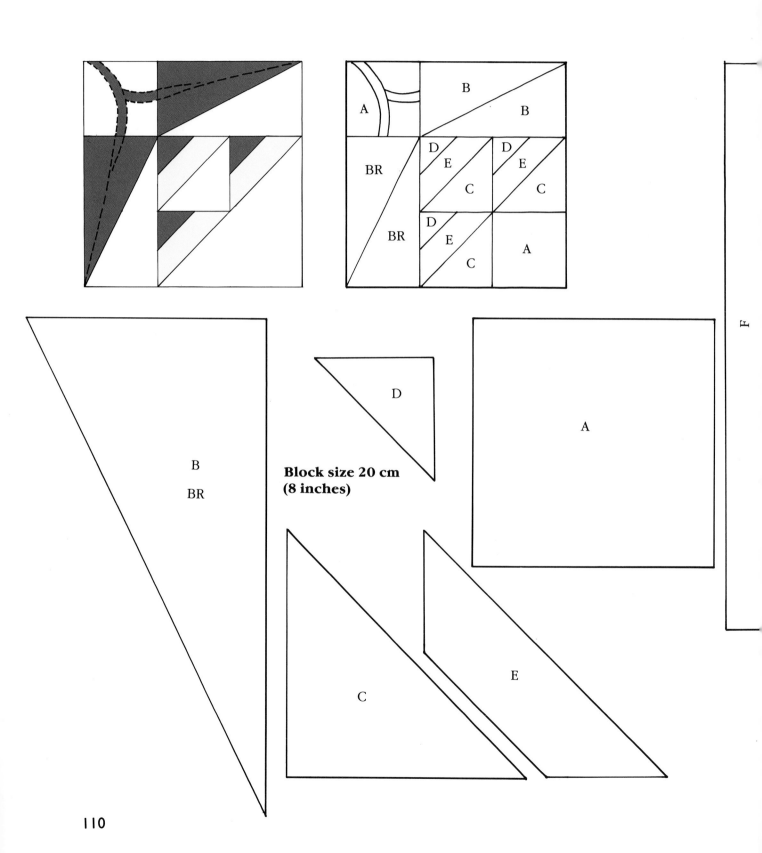

Block size 20 cm (8 inches)

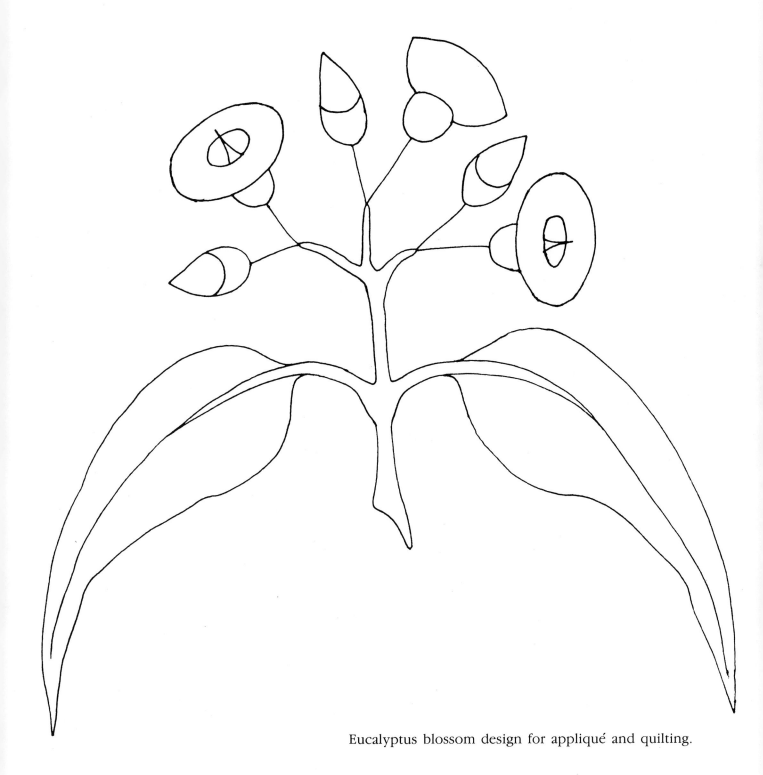

Eucalyptus blossom design for appliqué and quilting.

Eucalyptus blossom pattern 1 (continued)

Block size 30 cm (12 inches)

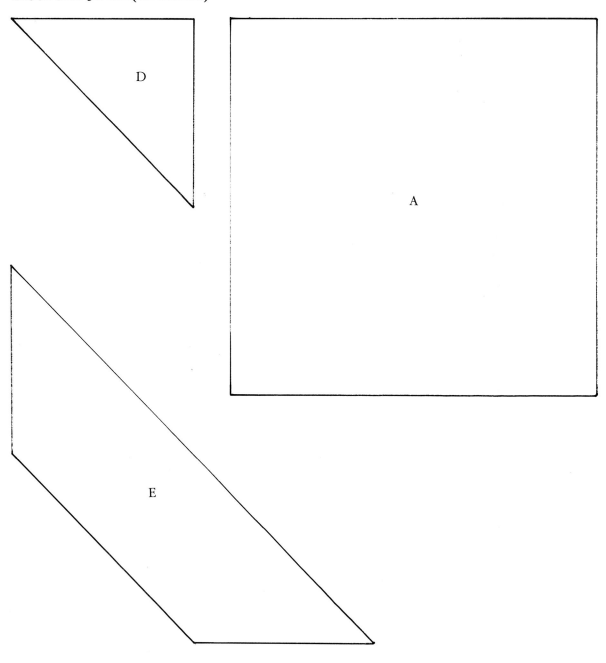

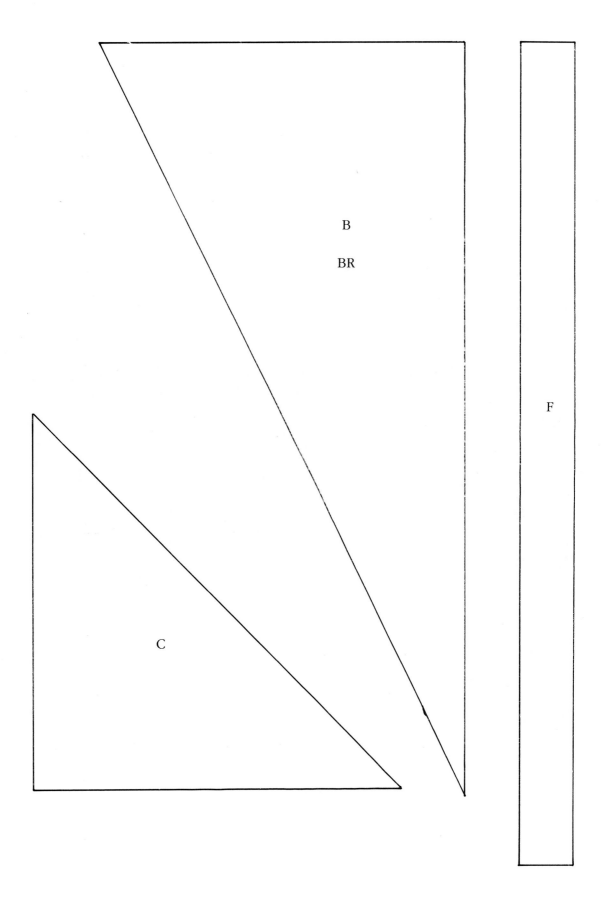

FLOWERING GUM QUILT
The rich colours of the Eucalyptus ficifolia have
been captured in this quilt. One pattern block,
Eucalyptus pattern 1, 3 × 3 units, has been
repeated for an overall quilt design.
CONSTRUCTION:
Machine pieced, hand quilted.
MEDIA:
Cotton homespuns.
SIZE:
290 cm × 210 cm.
MAKER:
Leslie Duffy.

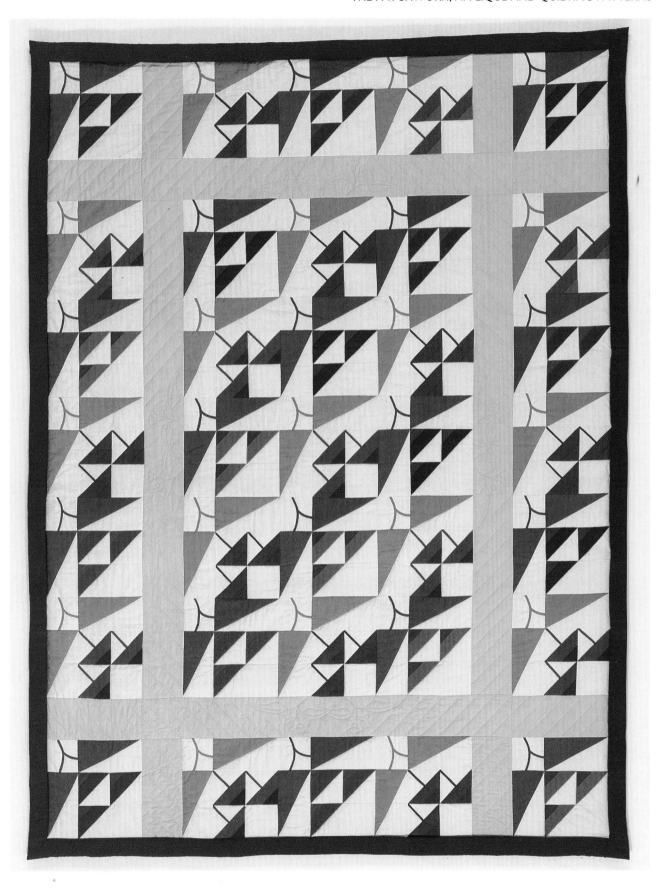

Eucalyptus blossom pattern 2

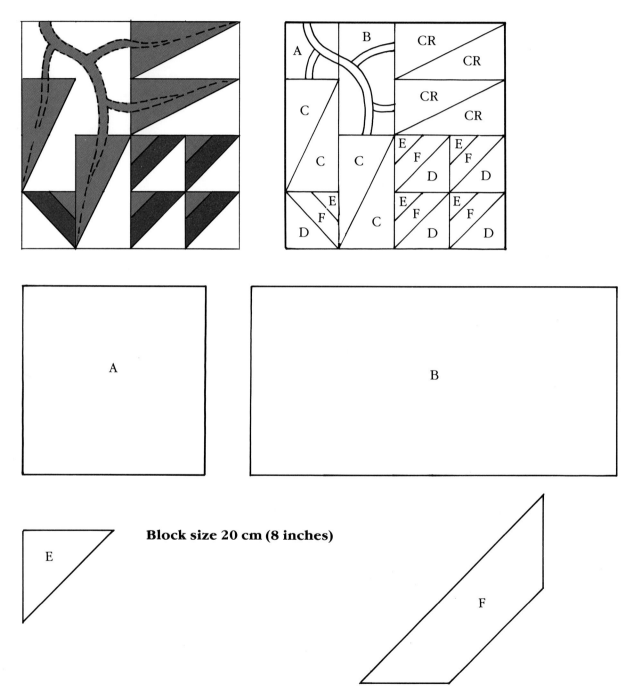

Block size 20 cm (8 inches)

Templates are also suitable to make up the many variations of the eucalyptus blocks. For example, the vertical arrangement on page 21 in the exploring patterns section.

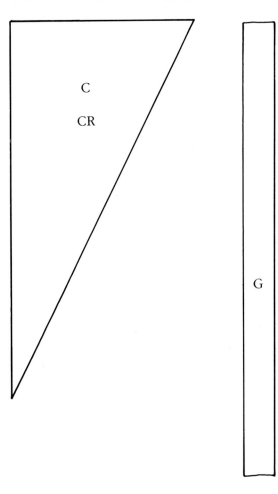

C

CR

G

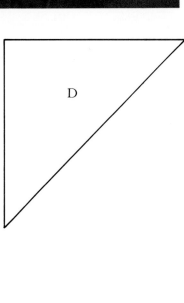

D

Eucalyptus blossom pattern 2 (continued)

Block size 30 cm (12 inches)

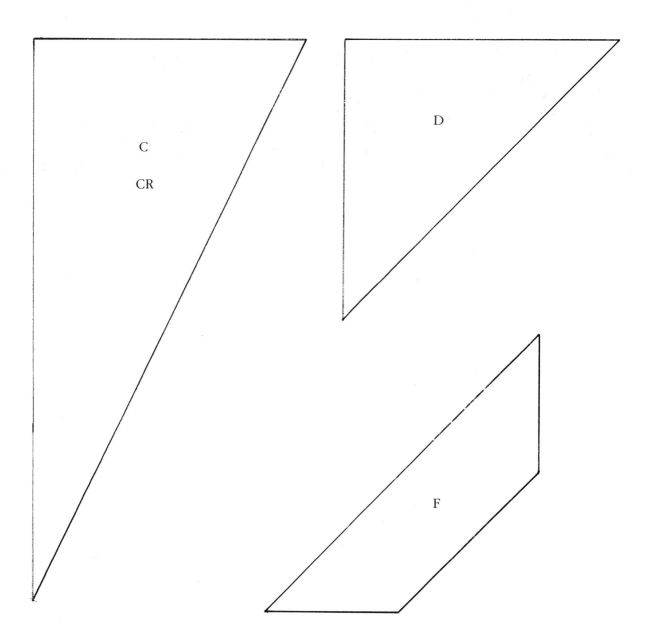

A

B

E

G

Eucalyptus leaf and moth design for appliqué or quilting

Eucalyptus blossom and moth border design
for appliqué or quilting

Christmas beetle

These large beetles appear around Christmas time, hence their common name. They are light brown with a beautiful metallic sheen as bright as Christmas tinsel. They may gather in enormous swarms on eucalypts, where they can cause severe defoliation.

Eucalyptus blossom — Rose of the West

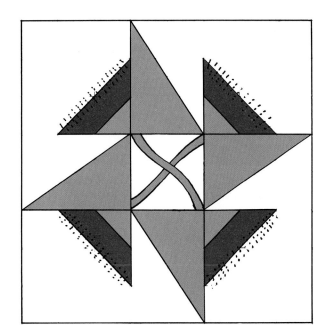

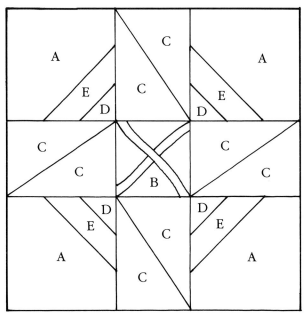

E. macrocarpa

ROSE OF THE WEST QUILT

"Soft grey polished cotton has been used to depict the grey white bloom on the leaves of this species of eucalypt. This eucalypt has extremely large rose-red flower you have to see to believe. This quilt is pieced entirely by hand using the English paper technique."

MEDIA:
Polished Cottons, prints and plain poly cottons.

SIZE:
132 cm × 166 cm.

MAKER:
Ida Wells.

Eucalyptus blossom — Rose of the west (continued)

Block size 20 cm (8 inches)

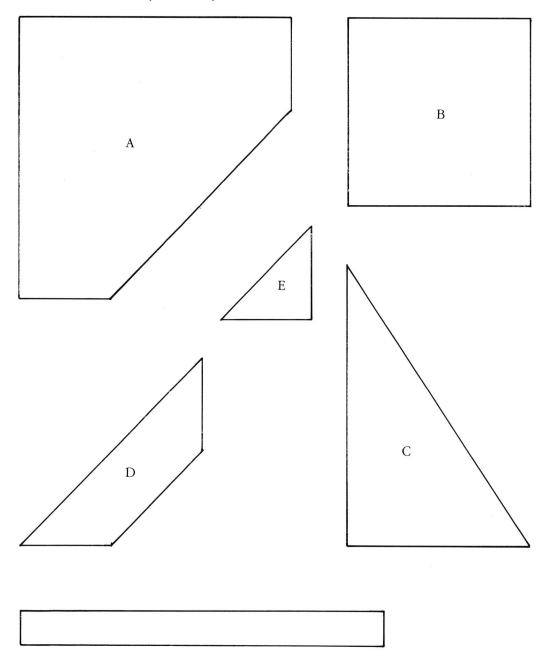

Eucalyptus blossom — Rose of the west (continued)

Block size 30 cm (12 inches)

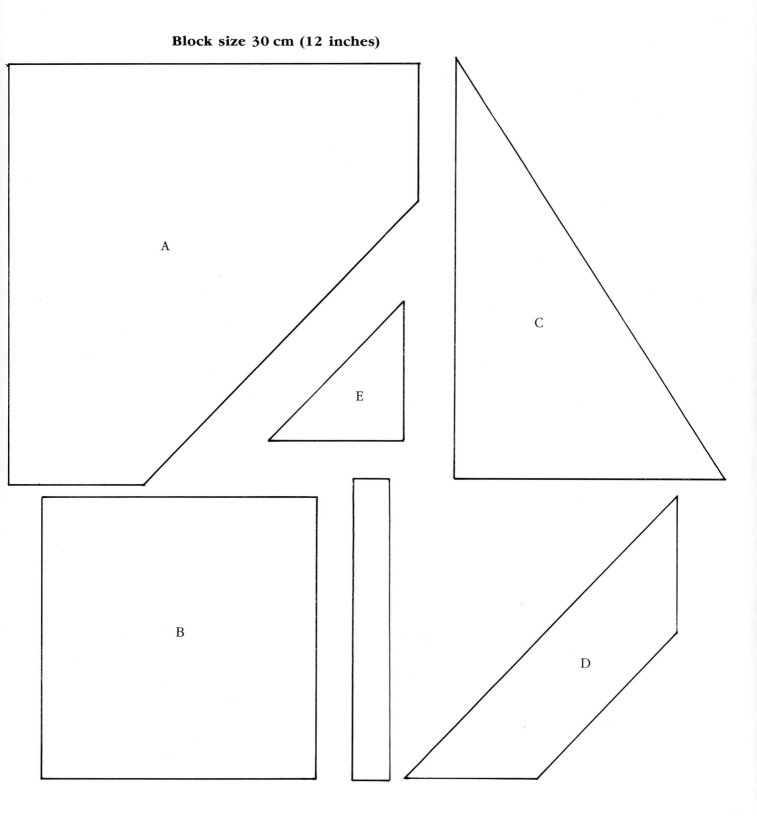

The buds, fruit and flowers are about life-size — it is one of the largest flowering eucalyptus species. A flower collected measured 9–10 cm across — it has to be seen to be believed. The stamens have large specks of pollen like French knots!

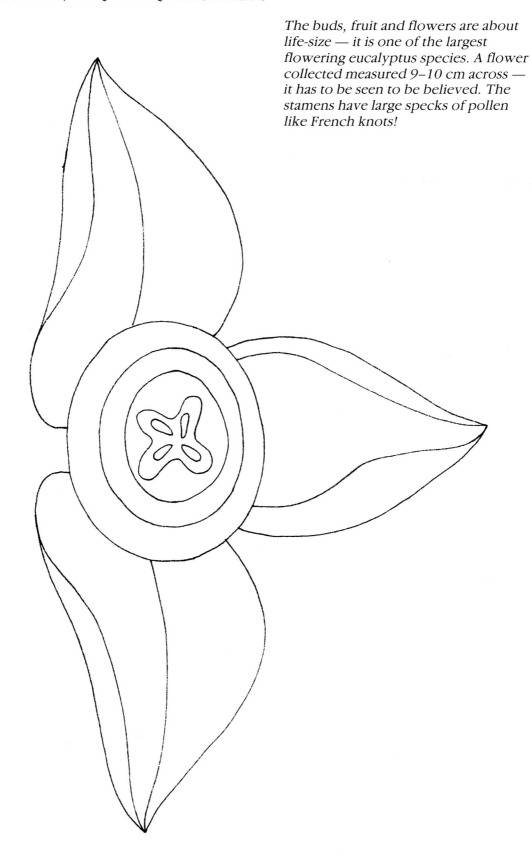

Rose of the west. *E. macrocarpa* quilting and appliqué pattern.

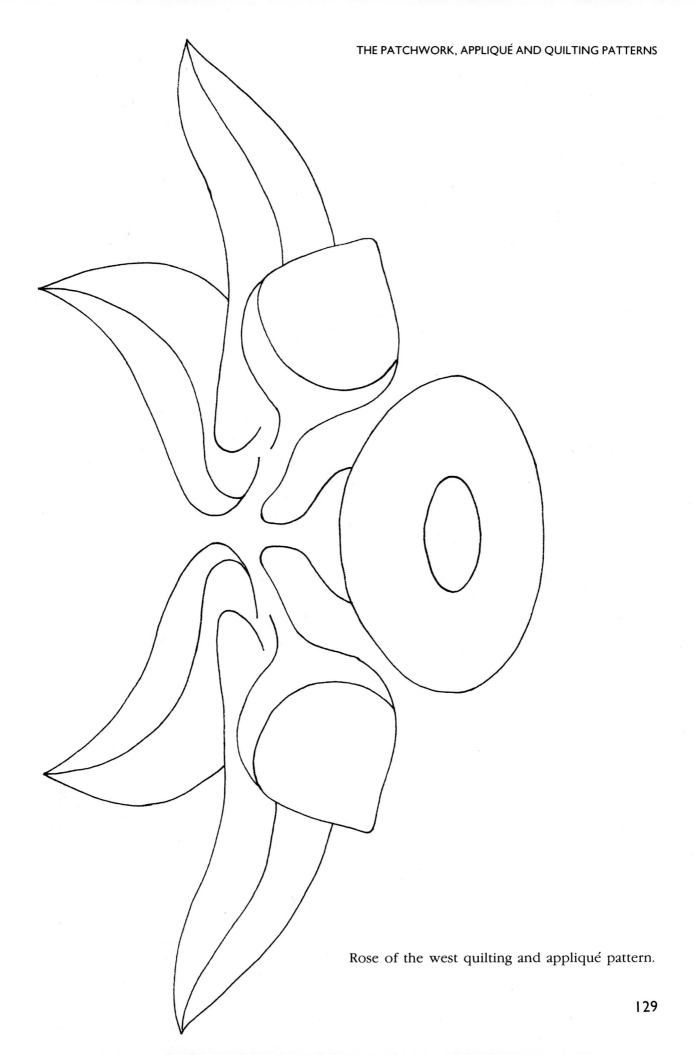

Rose of the west quilting and appliqué pattern.

Koala

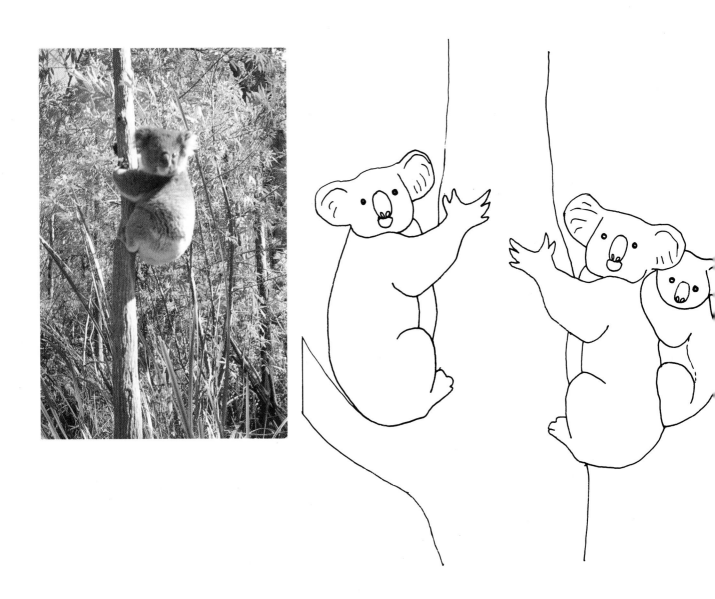

KOALA FAMILY QUILT

The placement of colour in this quilt gives another
dimension to this pattern. Koala footprints are
quilted around the border — The quilt is
unfinished.

CONSTRUCTION:
Machine pieced and appliqued hand quilted.

MEDIA:
Cotton Homespun.

SIZE:
110 cm × 100 cm.

MAKER:
Jennifer Hughes.

Koala

Note: For the koala without baby, trace koala following broken line to fill in back onto tracing paper, then reverse. Use the reverse image for pattern for koala family quilt.

Trace here for koala without baby.

Koala

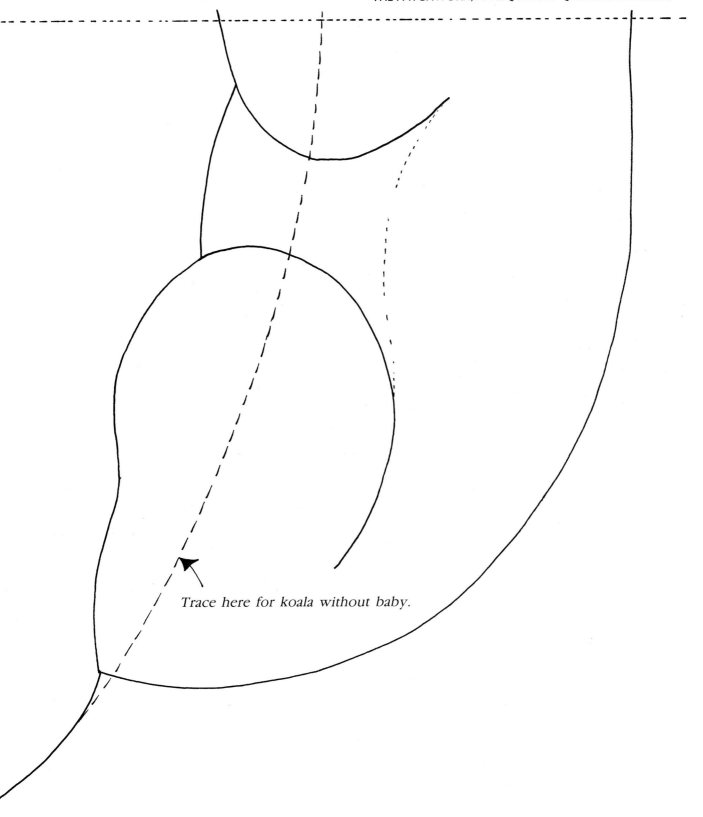

Trace here for koala without baby.

Boronia pattern 1

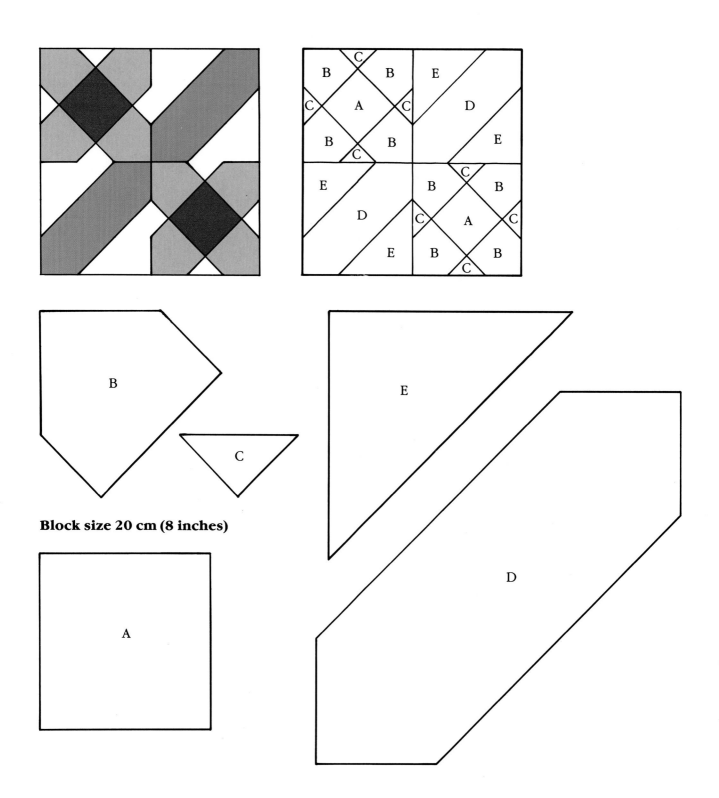

Block size 20 cm (8 inches)

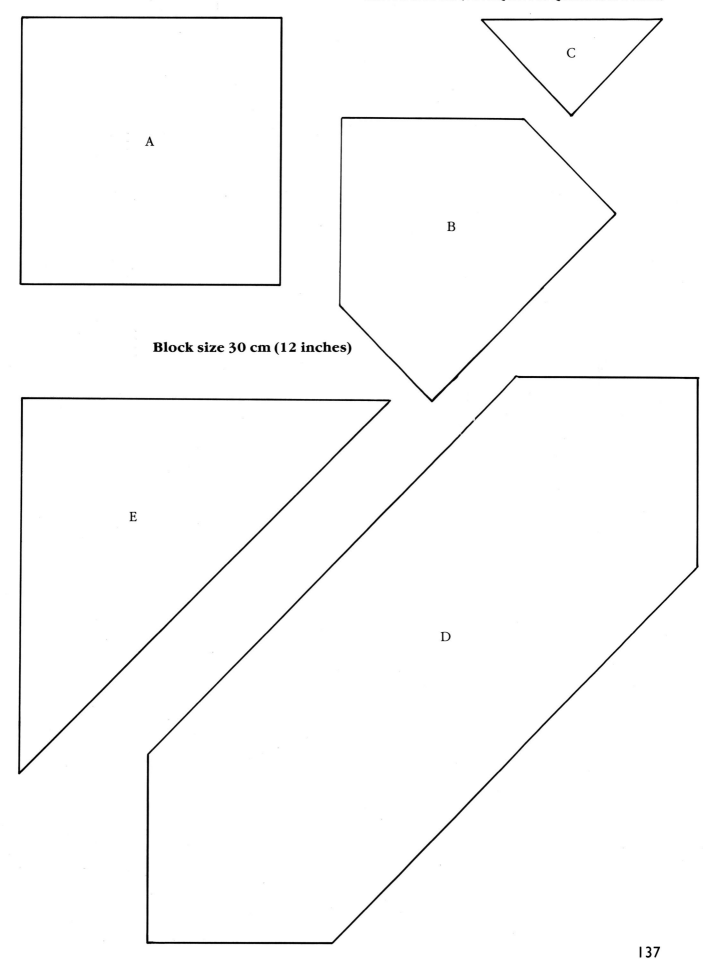

Block size 30 cm (12 inches)

Boronia pattern 2

Block size 20 cm (8 inches)

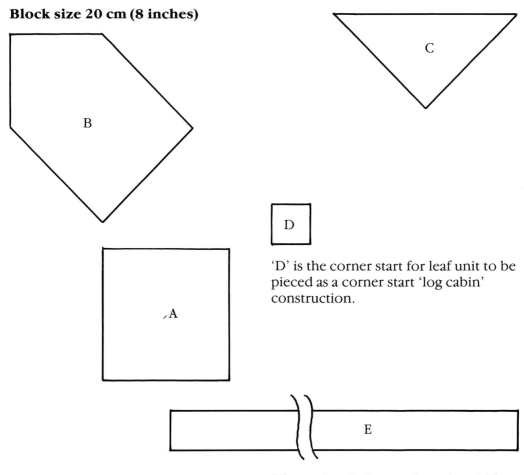

'D' is the corner start for leaf unit to be pieced as a corner start 'log cabin' construction.

'E' template indicates the strip width for the leaf and background unit of this block. This unit is pieced as a corner start 'log cabin' sequence. Sew the background fabric strip to the leaf fabric strip before commencing the corner start 'log cabin' piecing sequence.

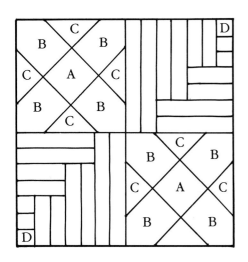

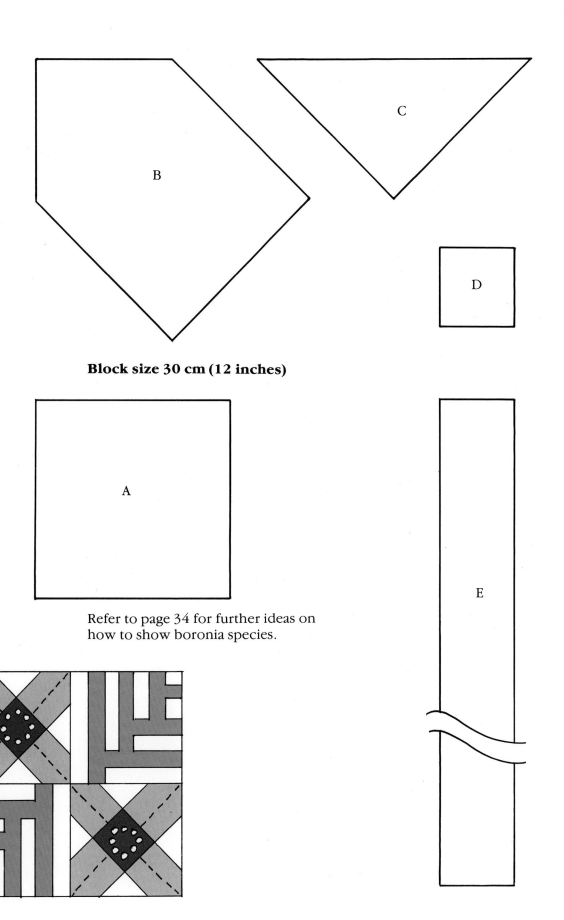

Block size 30 cm (12 inches)

Refer to page 34 for further ideas on
how to show boronia species.

Boronia

Boronia quilting and appliqué pattern

Heath

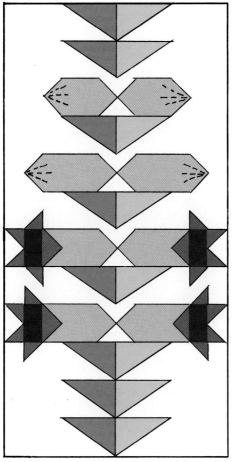

Pattern 1

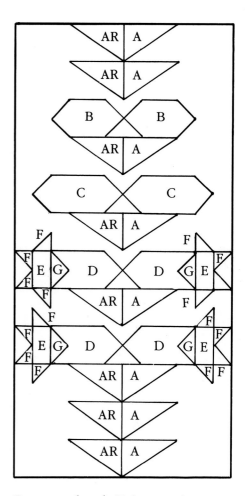

Common heath *E. impressia*

Heath

Block size 36 cm x 72 cm

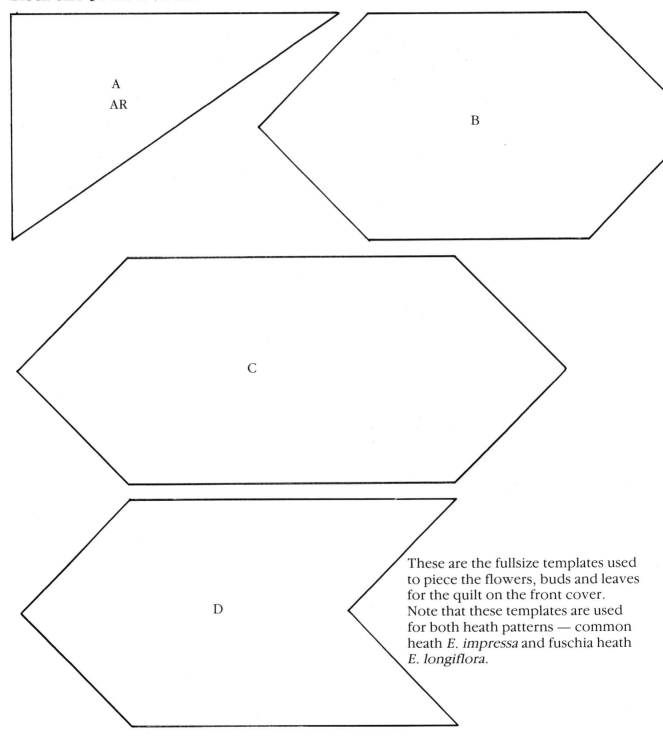

These are the fullsize templates used to piece the flowers, buds and leaves for the quilt on the front cover. Note that these templates are used for both heath patterns — common heath *E. impressa* and fuschia heath *E. longiflora*.

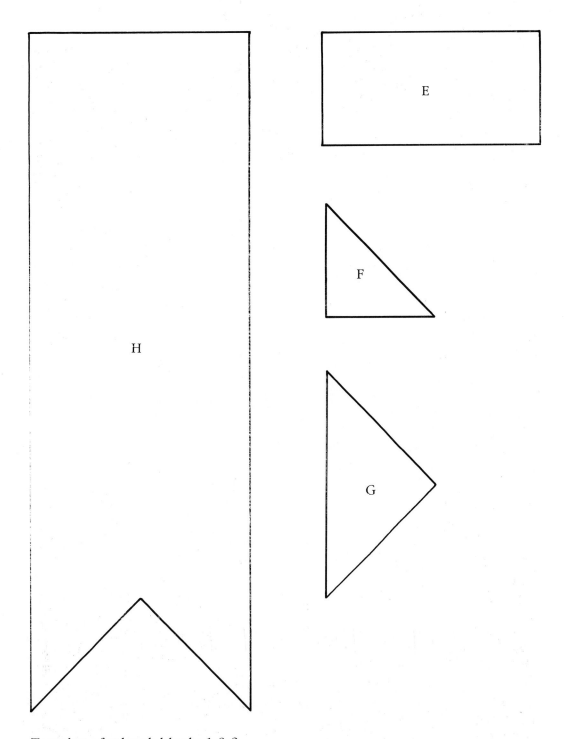

Templates for heath blocks 1 & 2

Note: The flowers are to be pieced then appliqued to the foundation block along with the buds and leaves: By doing this a 'softer' more realistic interpretation of the plant can be made. Appliqué stems could also be included.

PINK BUSH JEWELS

This quilt was made as a group project. The pieced background with the stems and leaves of the heath has been shaded with textile paints before the flowers were appliquéd in place. To obtain the desired shade of pink fabric for the flowers, printed fabrics were overdyed.

MEDIA:
Printed and plain cottons.

SIZE:
110 cm × 120 cm.

MAKERS:
Duckponds Quilting and Patchwork Group, Lara, Victoria.

Heath pattern 2

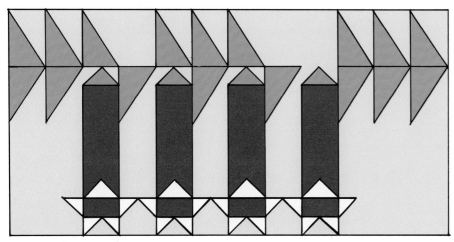

Pattern 2

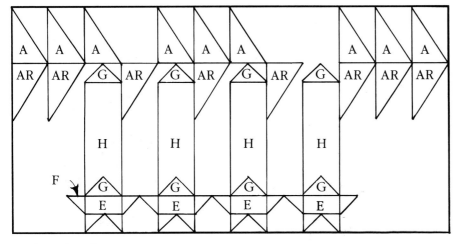

Fuchsia heath *E. longiflora*

FUCHSIA HEATH WINDCHEATER

Flowers have been highlighted with fabric paint before appliqueing in place, the leaves have been arranged up the arm and over the bodice to suggest the prostrate habit of this heath species.

CONSTRUCTION:
Machine Applique.

MEDIAS:
Cottons, silk taffeta.

MAKERS:
Anna Hughes, Deborah Brearley.

Note that some of the templates for patterns 1 and 2 are common.

E. longiflora

Full size patterns to make the heath
flowers, buds and leaves that decorate
the garment illustrated.

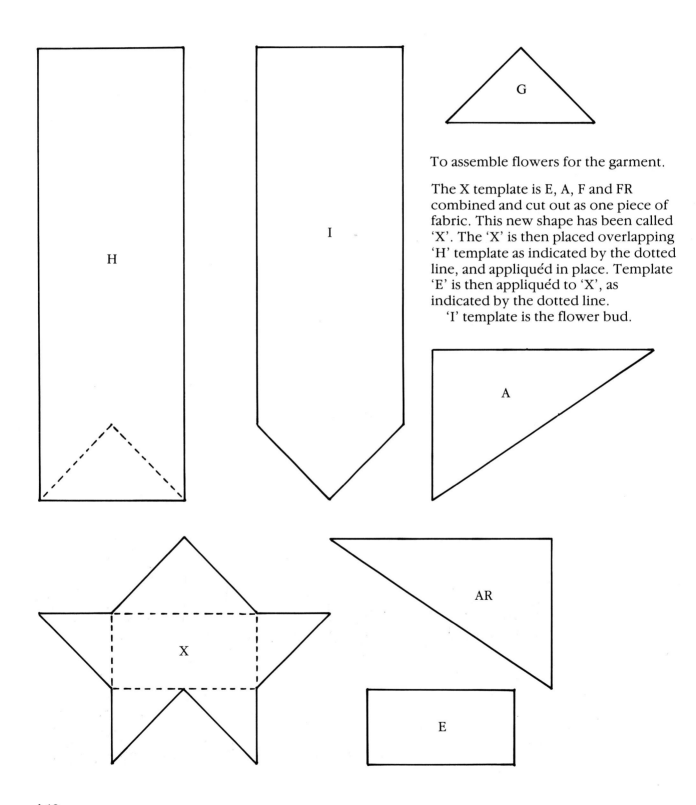

To assemble flowers for the garment.

The X template is E, A, F and FR
combined and cut out as one piece of
fabric. This new shape has been called
'X'. The 'X' is then placed overlapping
'H' template as indicated by the dotted
line, and appliquéd in place. Template
'E' is then appliquéd to 'X', as
indicated by the dotted line.
    'I' template is the flower bud.

Mint bush

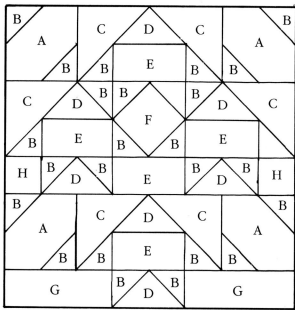

Pattern 1

Mint bush pattern 1

Block size 20 cm (8 inches)

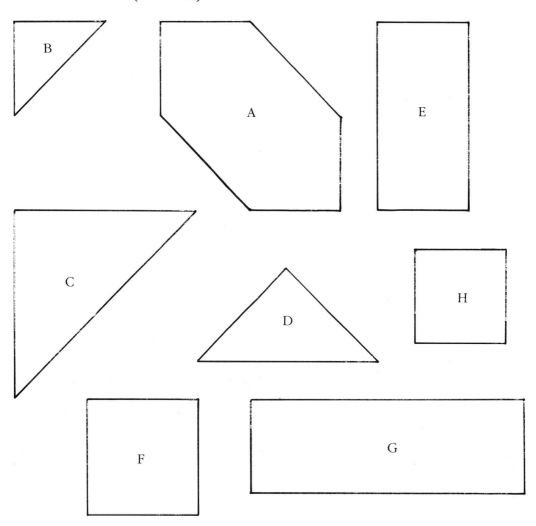

Note that both mint bush patterns 1 and 2 have templates in common.

Mint bush pattern 1 (continued)

Note that these patterns are used to
make up both mint bush patterns. Use
the additional two templates 'I' and 'J'
to complete mint bush pattern 2 block.

Block size 30 cm (12 inches)

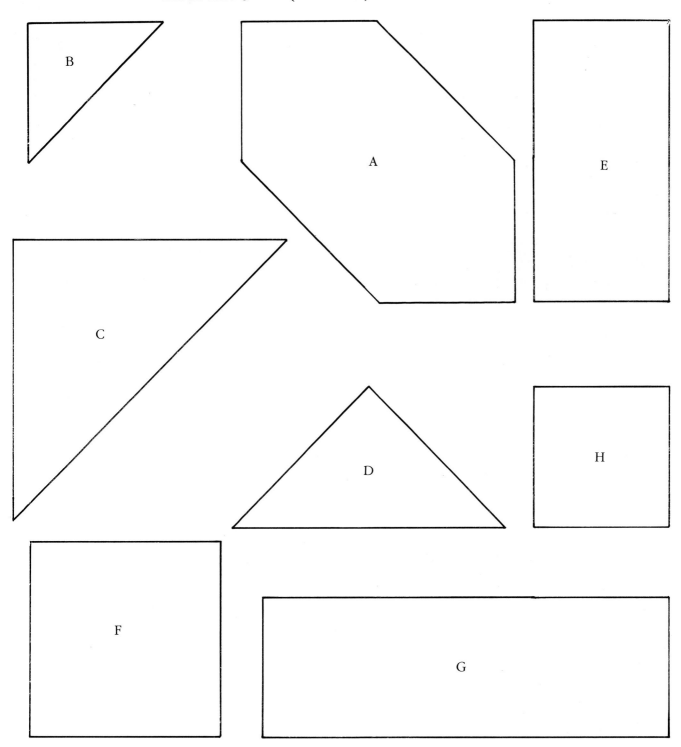

Mint bush pattern 2

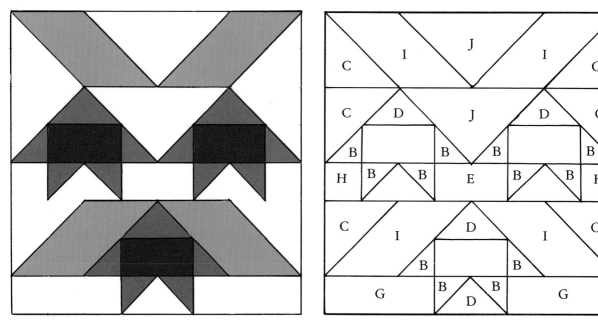

Pattern 2

Block size 20 cm (8 inches)

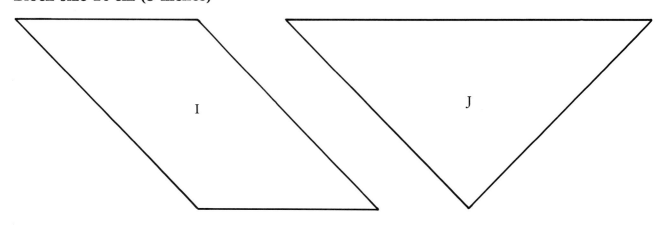

Block size 30 cm (12 inches)

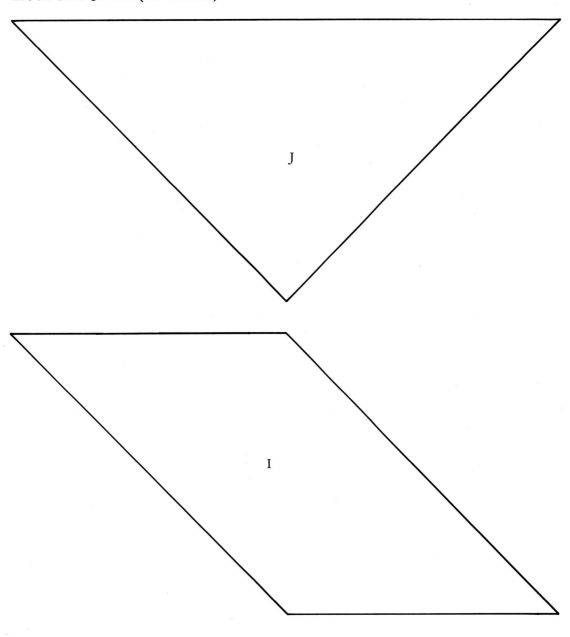

Mint bush

Mint bush quilting and appliqué pattern

Pink cockatoo

The pink cockatoo (*Cacatua leadbeateri*) resembles the well known sulphur crested cockatoo in shape, but it is smaller in size, around 36 cm. It is a delicate salmon-pink and white in colour with an eyecatching long crest with bands of bright red and yellow.

They are seen usually in pairs or small groups and can be often seen in the company of galahs. This beautiful bird is also known as the Major Mitchell cockatoo, after one of our early explorers, Sir Thomas Mitchell (1772–1855).

Pink cockatoo

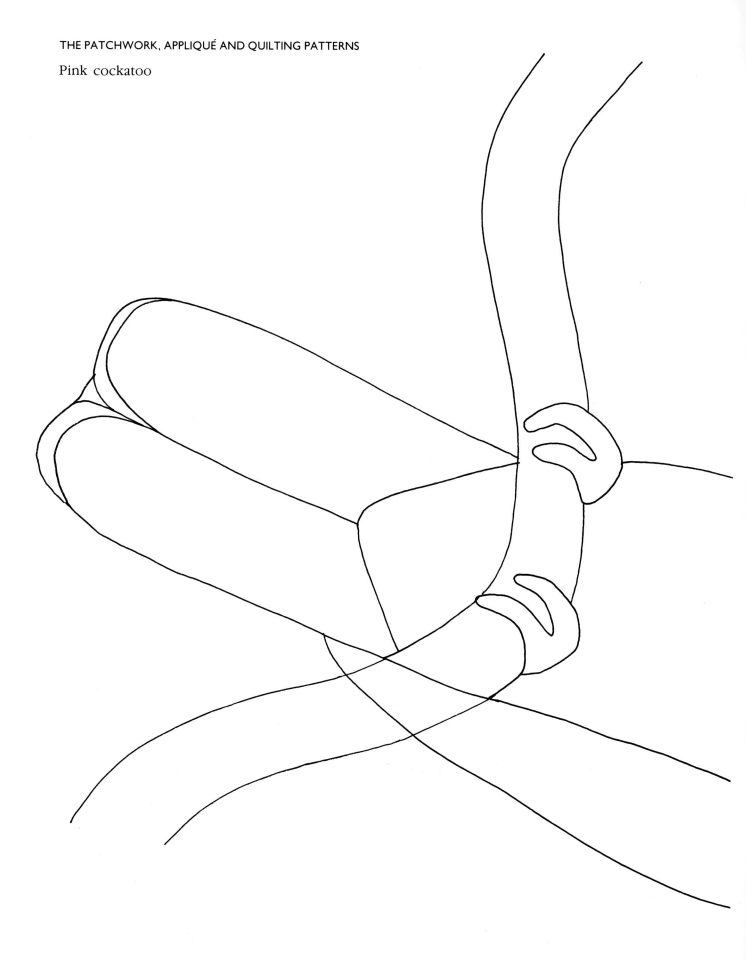

Pink cockatoo

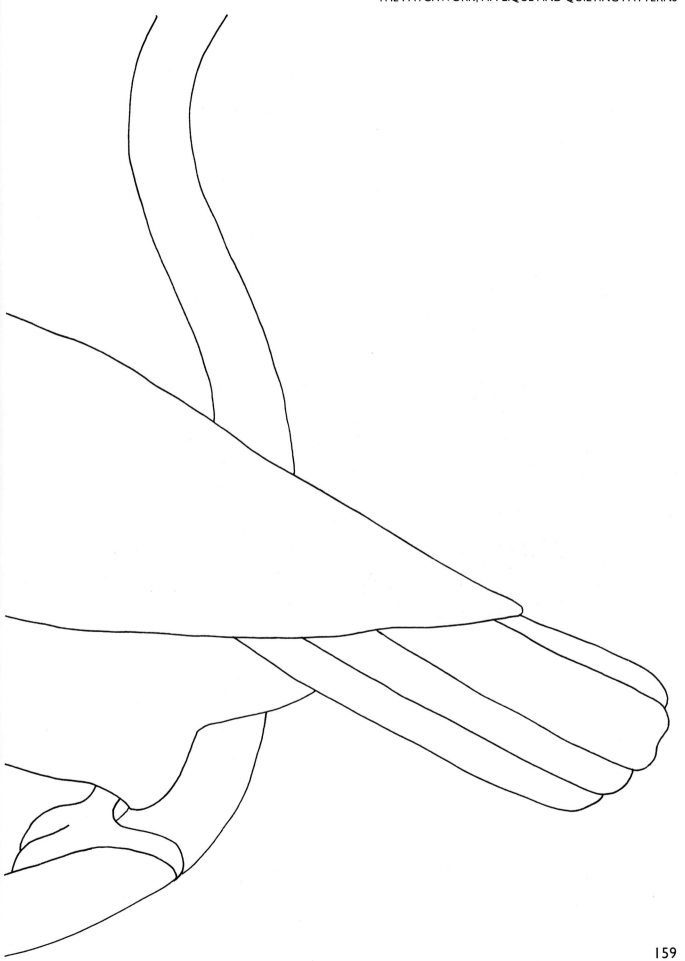

Cockatiel

The cockatiel (*Nymphicus hollandicus*) with its distinctive colouring is widespread and common throughout the country. Its general plumage is grey, the males have a face, crest and throat of yellow and an apricot-orange ear patch. The female has a paler yellow face, a grey crest and a duller coloured ear patch. The birds have long tails and a large white shoulder patch on their pointed wings. These lovable birds are often kept as pets; they can learn to whistle and imitate a few words.

Cockatiel

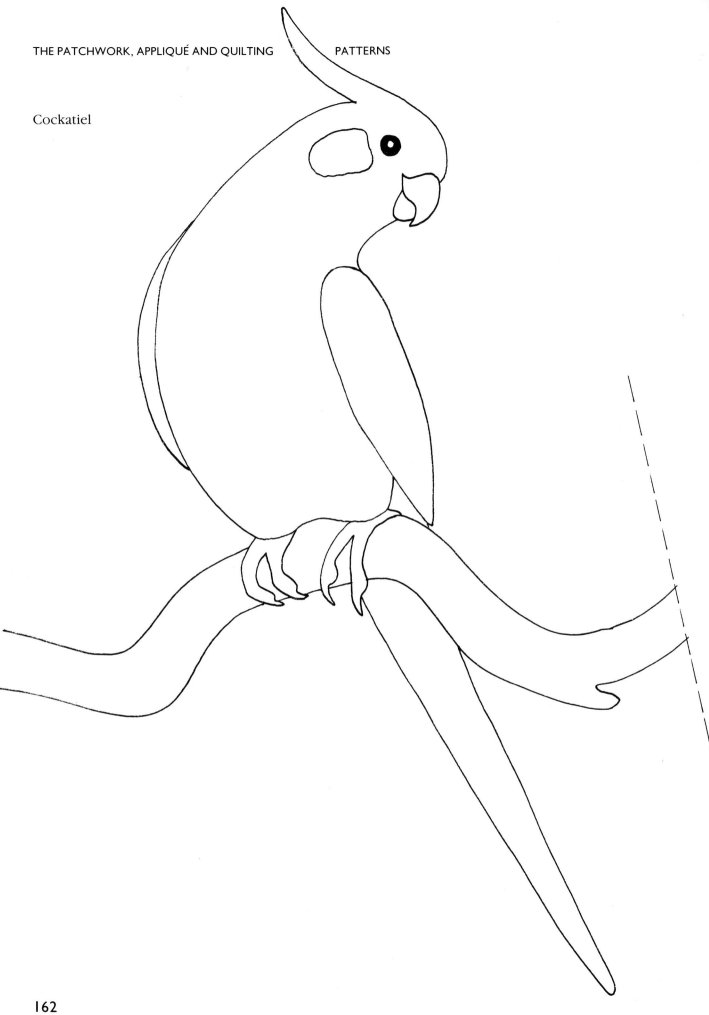

Eastern rosellas

The eastern rosella (*Platycercus eximius*), about 30 cm in length, is a well known parrot because it is often used as a trademark. It has a red head and upper breast, white cheeks and yellow to leaf-green body. Outer tail feathers are pale to leaf green, inner tail feathers are blue. It feeds on seeds and blossoms and is often regarded as a nuisance because it is particularly fond of cultivated fruit. It will not eat a complete fruit, but instead likes to take sample bites out of a number, making itself rather unpopular!

Eastern Rosella

Eastern rosella 1

Eastern rosella 2

Black shouldered kite

The black shouldered kite (*Elanus notatus*), about 36 cm in length, is found throughout the mainland and can often be seen hovering in search of small mammals, birds, reptiles and insects. The body and tail are white, and its grey wings feature a broad black shoulder patch. It has a large orange-red eye surrounded by black, a black beak and legs and feet of yellow. The birds perch singly or in family groups in top branches of dead trees. They choose a tall thick-foliaged tree to build their nest of sticks lined with leaves. They raise up to four young.

We tended and 'baby sat' a juvenile kite (they are brown-tan on head, breast and back) for some time. This ferocious looking youngster had come off second-best in a territorial fight with some magpies. We were very happy to release it because of the difficulty of keeping up a supply of mice which he preferred to mince steak!

Black shouldered kite – male bird

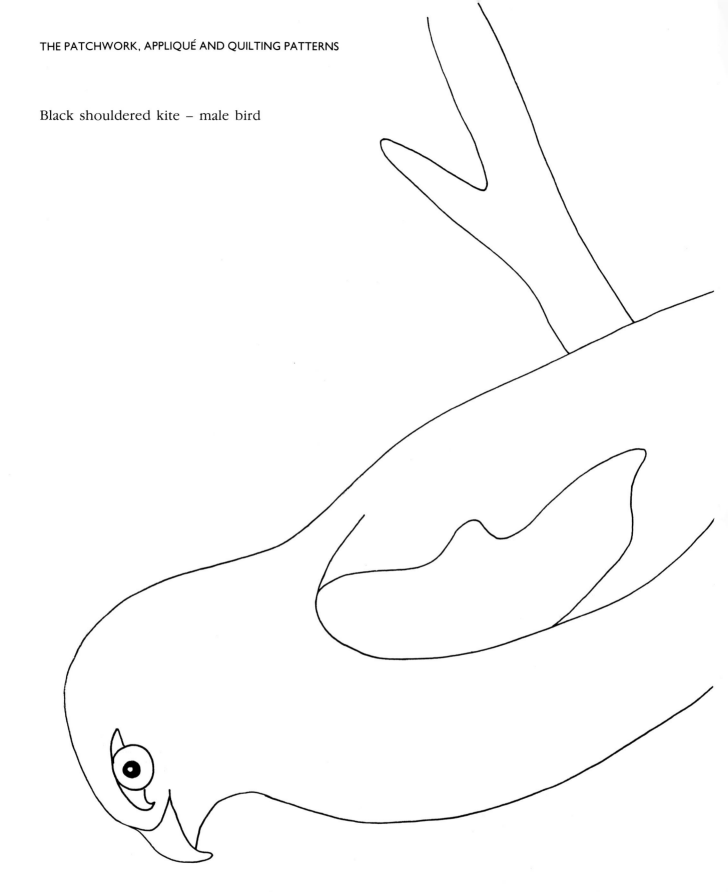

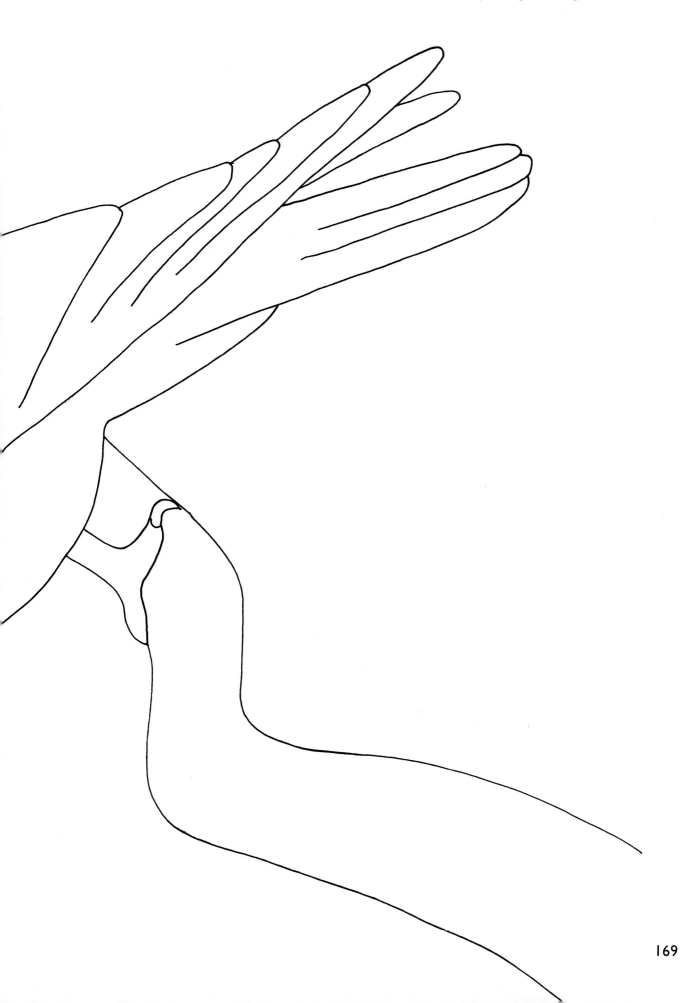

Black shouldered kite – female bird

Black shouldered kite – juvenile bird

Marsupial mouse

This is one of our many native mice. The pattern has been included so that the black shouldered kite, if used for a quilt, has something to stalk. Hide the poor little fellow in a border!!

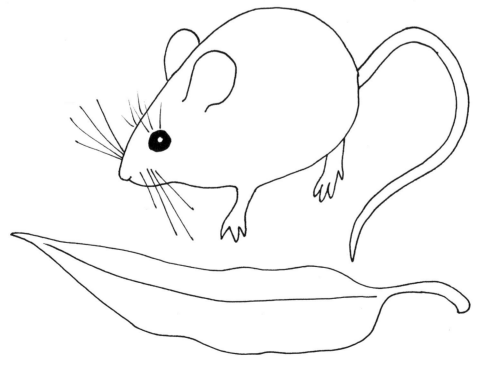

Hovea

Hoveas (*Papilionaceae*) are erect shrubs from 30 cm to one metre in height. They are found in all states of Australia. The typical pea-shaped flowers in shades of blue and purple grow in clusters up the stem of the plant, alternating with the slender green leaves.

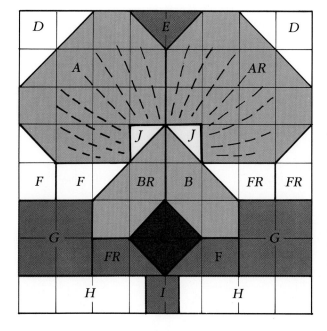

Hovea species

Refer to page 35 for further ideas on depicting hovea species.

Hovea

Block size 20 cm (8 inches)

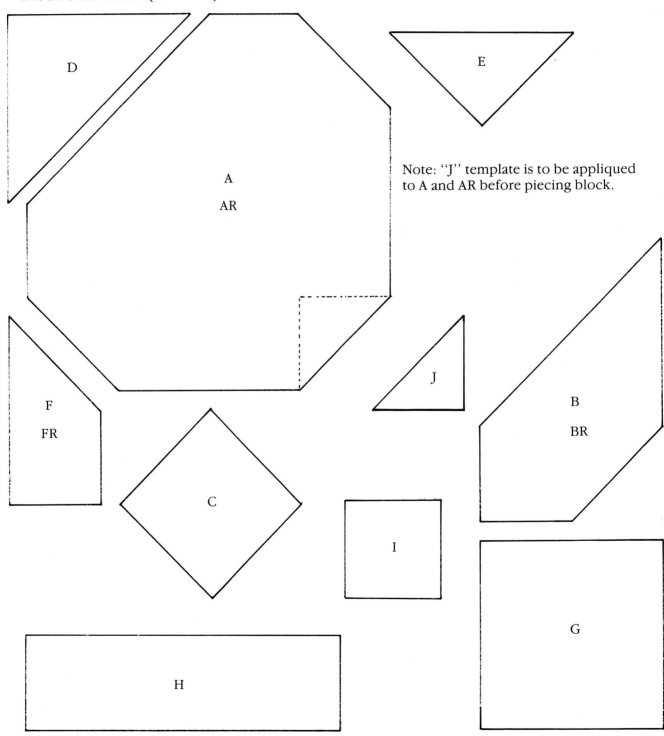

Note: "J" template is to be appliqued to A and AR before piecing block.

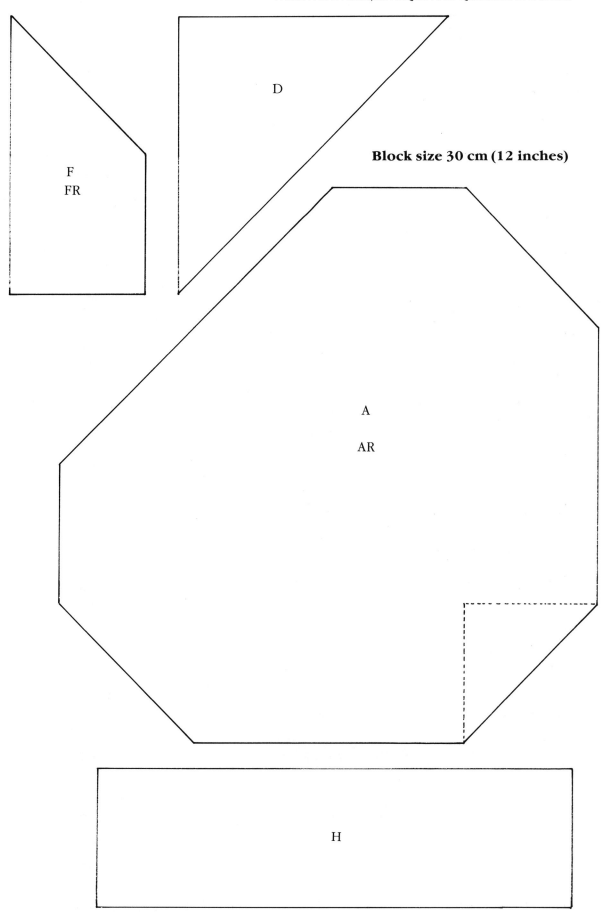

Block size 30 cm (12 inches)

F
FR

D

A
AR

H

Hovea (continued)

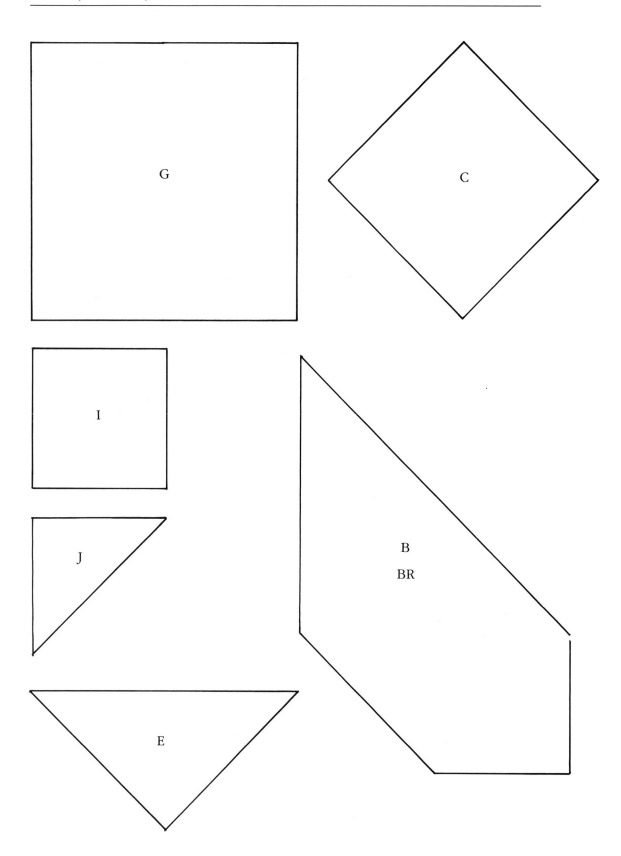

Note: J template is to be appliqued to A and AR before piecing block.

Native orchids

The native orchids are some of our most delicate flowers. Their variety of form and colour, as well as their varied habitats, make them a fascinating plant. Some grow in tropical areas clinging to trees and rocks, some grow in flat open areas.

One of our most well-known orchids is *Dendrobium bigibbum* — the Cooktown orchid, the floral emblem of Queensland. The plant grows on stunted scrubby trees and rocks in elevated areas of north Queensland. The flowers of white, lilac, mauve or magenta appear in clusters of up to twenty blooms. The blooms, 3 to 5 cm across on stems, are attached to long arching canes, green to reddish purple and up to 120 cm in length. Leaves are thin, 5 to 15 cm long, and green with sometimes reddish markings.

To depict the plant in a naturalistic way, refer to the diagram. First piece the flowers, then appliqué them along with the stems to a foundation which may be pieced to include the leaves. Alternatively, appliqué the leaf shapes in place.

The flower can also be presented in block form. The pattern for a 30 cm (12 inch) and 20 cm (8 inch) block appears on pages 181, 182 and 183.

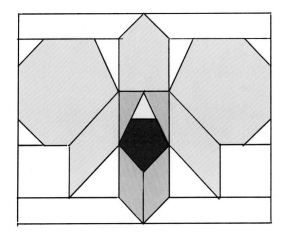

Native orchid flower
10 x 8 units

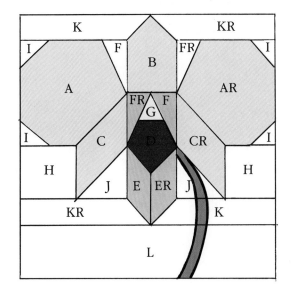

The flower could also be presented in block form. For a square block, simply add an extra row of units top and/or bottom to the pattern to bring it up to 10 x 10 units. Appliqué a stem in place if you wish.
Pattern for a 30 cm and 20 cm block, pages 180 to 183.

179

Cooktown orchid

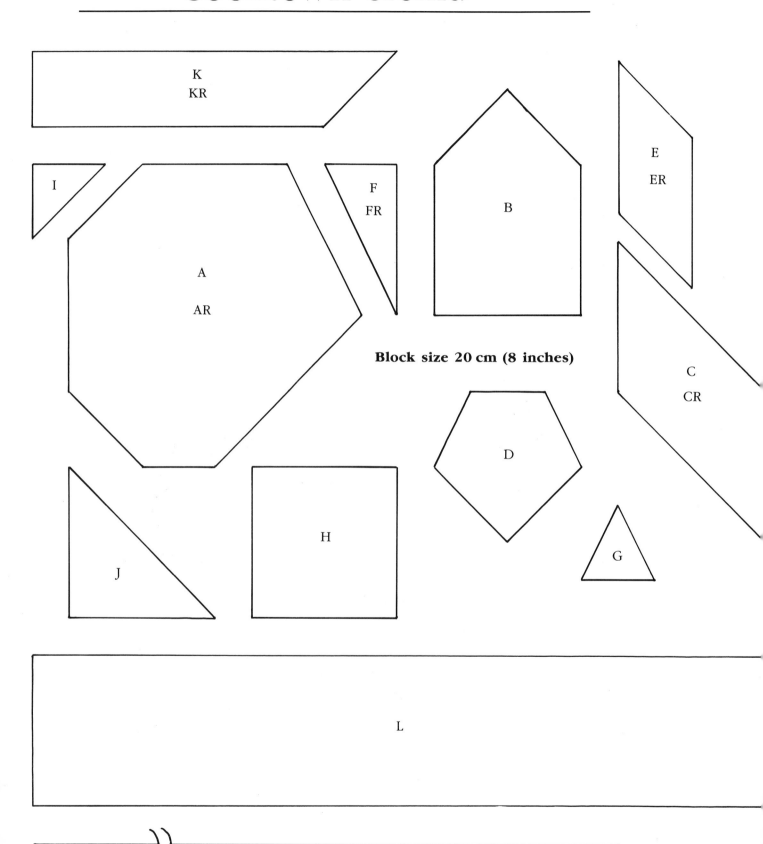

K
KR

I

F
FR

A
AR

E
ER

B

Block size 20 cm (8 inches)

C
CR

D

H

J

G

L

Width of bias strip for stems

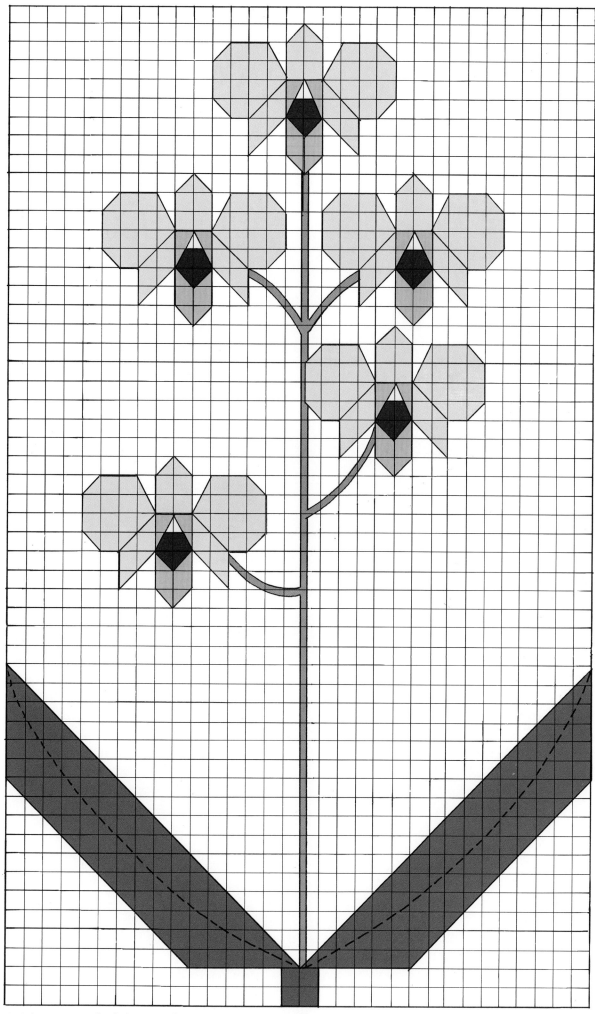

Cooktown orchid depicted in a naturalistic way.

Cooktown orchid (continued)

Block size 30 cm (12 inches)

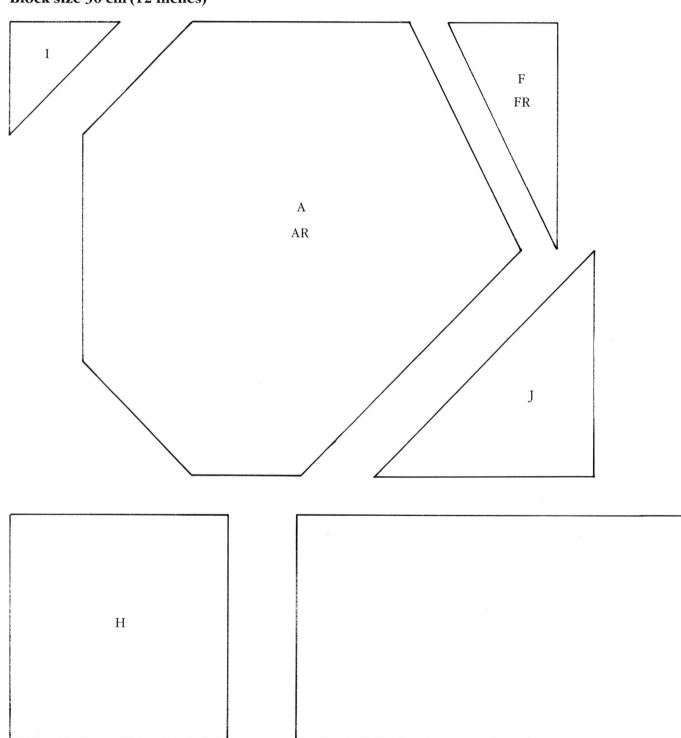

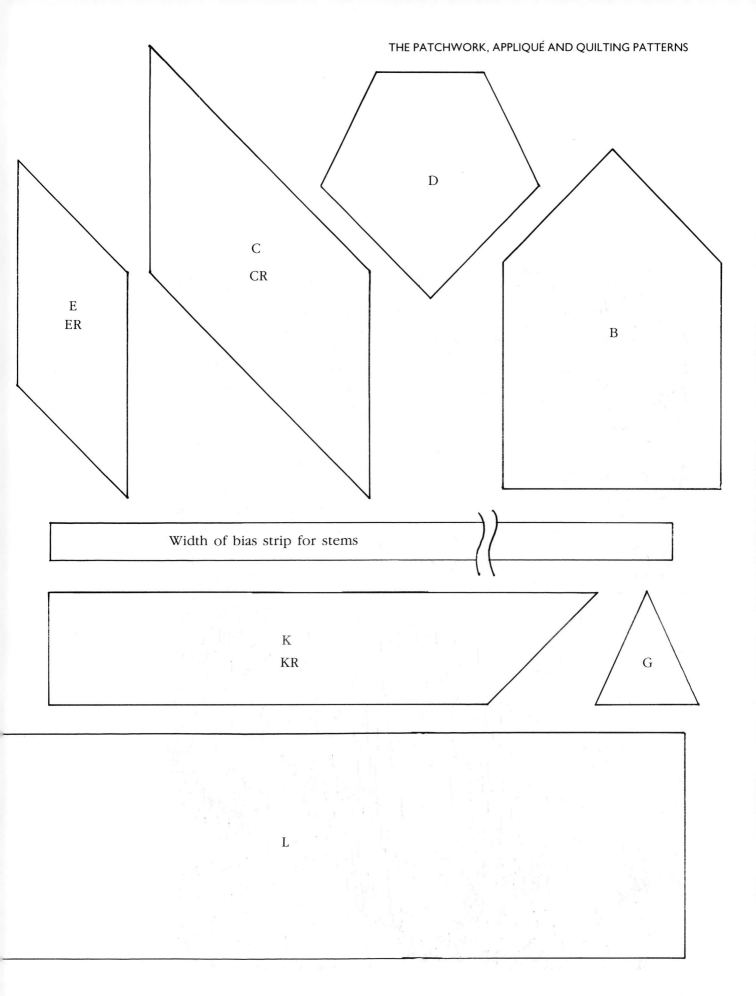

D

C
CR

E
ER

B

Width of bias strip for stems

K
KR

G

L

Pink rock orchid

The pink rock orchid (*Dendrobium kingianum*) is another of our delicate native orchids. It is found on the coast from New South Wales to Queensland. It is a rock-dweller and it can cling to almost bare rocks. In places, it carpets rock ledges where it grows with ferns and mosses under fairly wet conditions. It is from pure white in colour through pinky red to deep red, and ranges in size from smaller than a thumbnail to 4 cm across. A number of flowers grow on a stem in a similar fashion to that of the Cooktown.

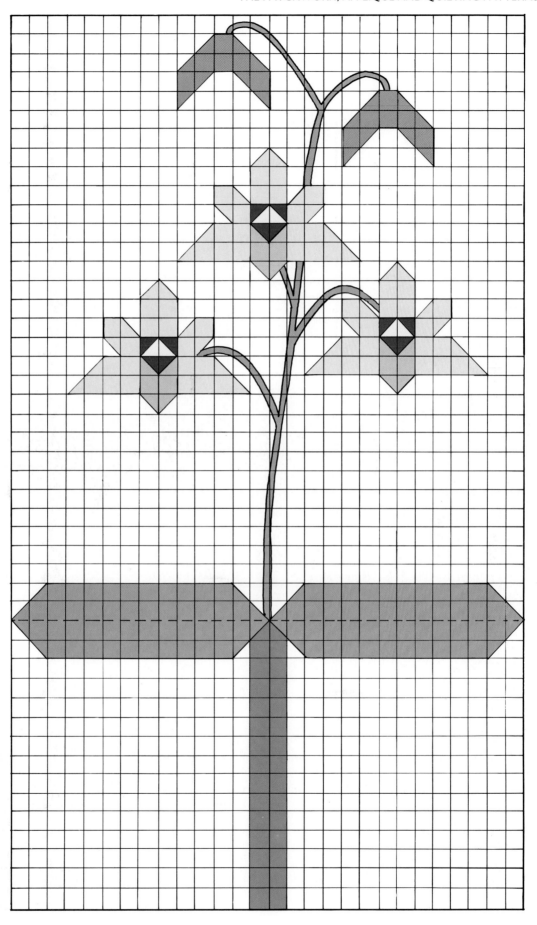

Pink rock orchid (continued)

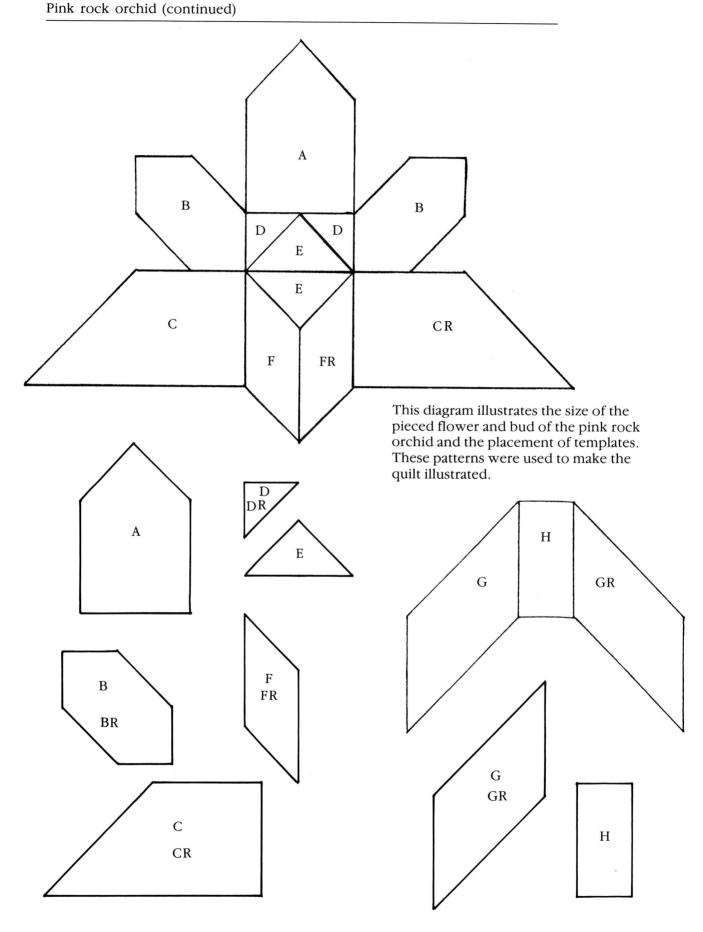

This diagram illustrates the size of the pieced flower and bud of the pink rock orchid and the placement of templates. These patterns were used to make the quilt illustrated.

PINK ROCK ORCHIDS

The fabrics for the orchid flowers have been hand-painted to capture the subtle colouring and markings of these delicate flowers. The bud motif has been used to make a border which frames the realistic depiction of the species. The background has been coloured with textile paints before the orchid has been appliquéd in place.

CONSTRUCTION
Hand pieced, hand quilted
SIZE
110 cm x 100 cm
MAKER
Dot Caple

Pink rock orchid.

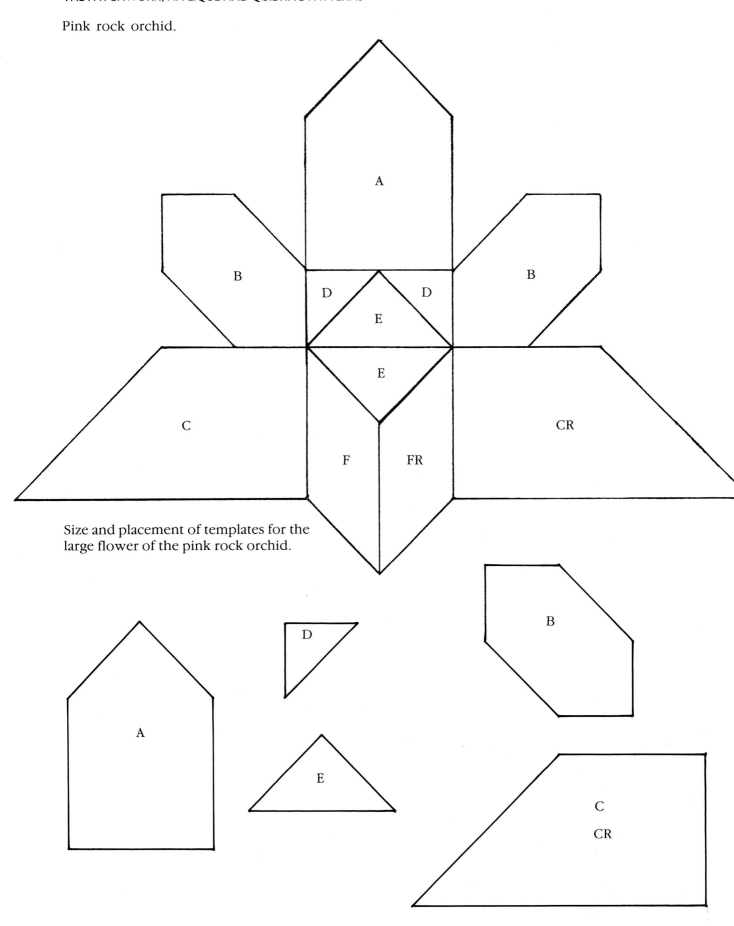

Size and placement of templates for the
large flower of the pink rock orchid.

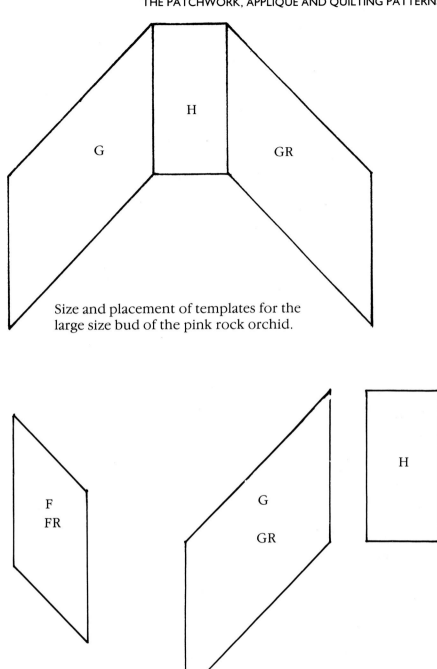

Size and placement of templates for the large size bud of the pink rock orchid.

These patterns for making templates to piece the flower and buds of the pink rock orchid were used in conjunction with the small flower and bud patterns to portray this orchid in the quilt illustrated on page 187.

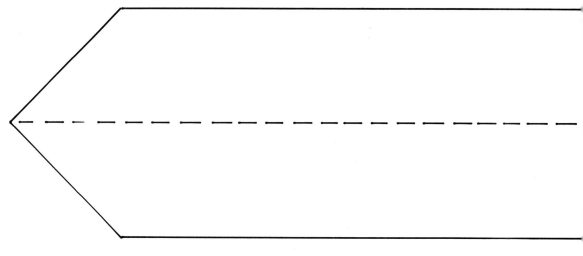

Pink rock orchid   small leaf — stem

dotted line indicates a row of quilting to suggest the vein and crease of the orchid leaf.

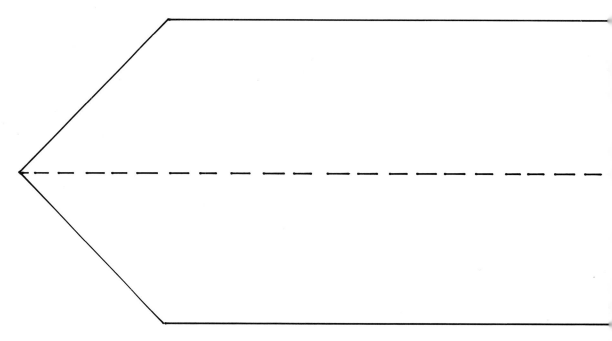

Pink rock orchid   large leaf — stem

The large leaf was used in the quilt illustrating the pink rock orchid on page 187.

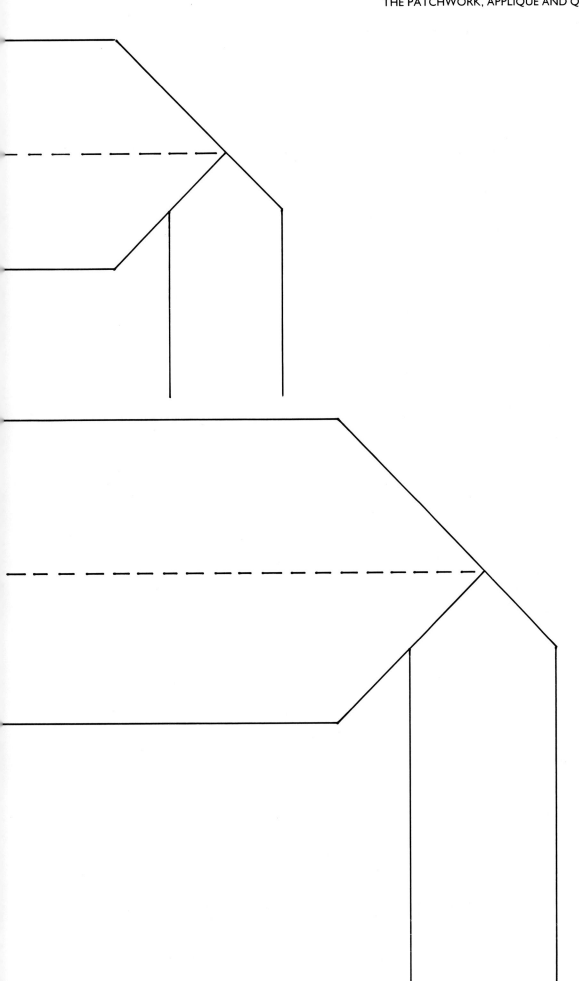

Spotted sun orchid

The sun orchids (*Thelymitras*) are among the most beautiful of the ground orchids. They open and close with the sun, hence their common name. The flower(s) precede the leaves which rise annually from an underground tuber. Their colours vary greatly — yellows, pinks, blues. One of the most common is the spotted sun orchid (*T. ixioides*). It occurs in all states and is found on flats and tablelands and summits of ridges. It is usually a blue-purple in colour, but may be pink or any shade between, marked with dots of a deeper shade. The flowers, 3 to 4 cm across, grow on a long upright stem; there may be from 2 to 15 flowers per stem. The leaves, long and grass-like usually appear after the flowering.

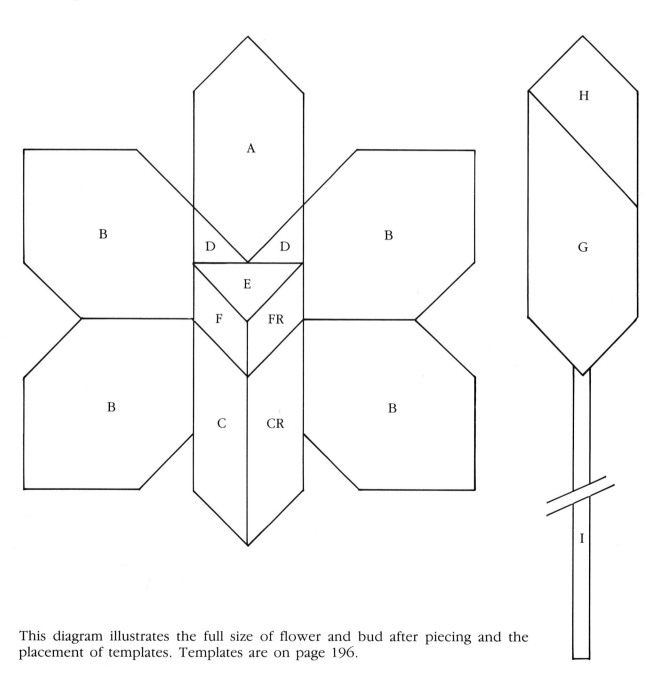

This diagram illustrates the full size of flower and bud after piecing and the placement of templates. Templates are on page 196.

Give careful consideration
to fabric choices when depicting
these orchids. Perhaps even
consider using fabric markers
or dyes to suggest their spots
or stripes.

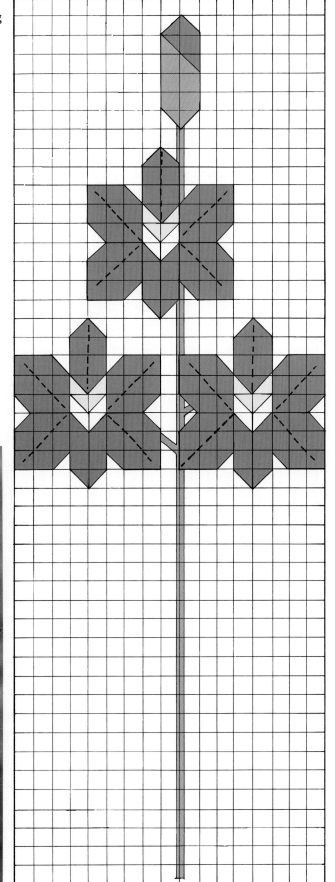

Veined sun orchid

The veined sun orchid (*T. venosa*) has bright indigo blue flowers (sometimes pink) striped with darker veins. The flowers, one to 10 in number and up to 5 cm across, appear on stems which may be 45 cm tall. It usually grows on swampy ground in the southern part of Australia.

When depicting these orchids, try and capture their character. They are very dainty and their subtle textures are worthy of careful fabric selection.

Use the Cooktown orchid pattern as a guide to drafting the template shapes for the pink rock orchid and the sun orchids. I envisage these patterns being pieced, then appliquéd to a foundation. It would be easier to capture their delicate nature and growing habits with curved appliquéd stems and clusters of pieced flowers in this way.

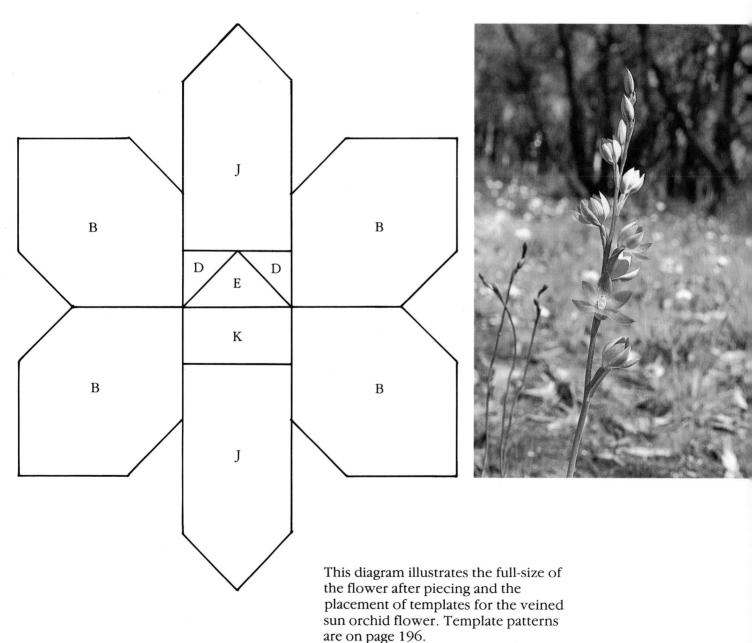

This diagram illustrates the full-size of the flower after piecing and the placement of templates for the veined sun orchid flower. Template patterns are on page 196.

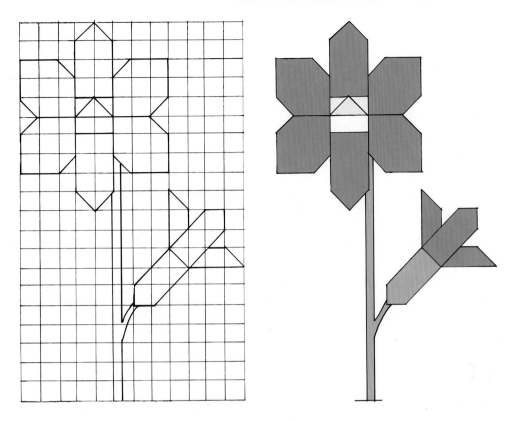

The veined sun orchid (*Thelymitra venosa*)

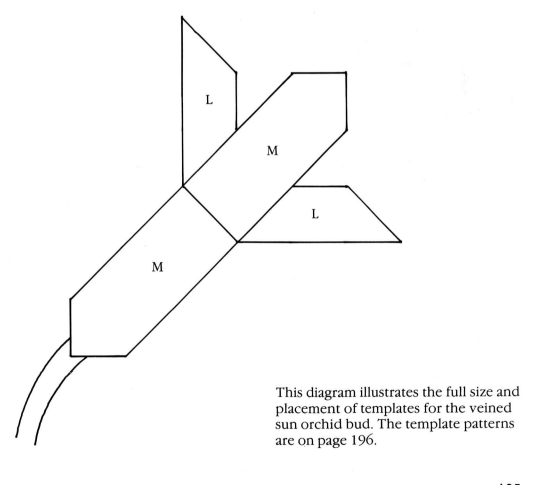

This diagram illustrates the full size and placement of templates for the veined sun orchid bud. The template patterns are on page 196.

Templates for spotted and veined sun orchids.

For spotted sun orchid use templates   A, B, C, CR, D, E, F, FR, G, H, I.

For veined sun orchid use   B, D, E, I, J, K, L, M.

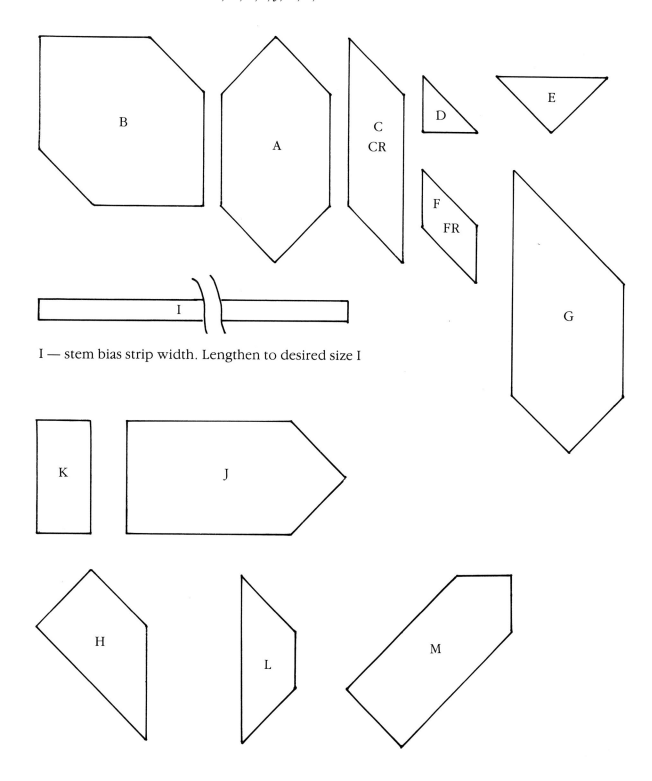

I — stem bias strip width. Lengthen to desired size I

When depicting the smaller species of flora, try and capture their charm. I find it disappointing to see some of our small delicate flowers, for example orchids, hoveas etc., depicted in the same size and along-side callistemon or some of our larger flowers.

If you wish to make a quilt or the like featuring a favourite plant, take a little time researching its habitat, size, colourings etc. — a more authentic and more interesting quilt will be the result.

Take a little time to discover our flowers — so many of them are tiny and often overlooked. Once you discover them you will realise their subtle beauty and colouring and you will find much inspiration and guidance in colour and fabric selection for your appliqué, piecing and embroidery.

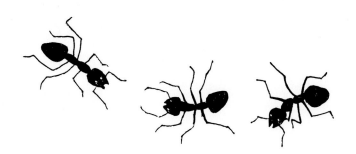

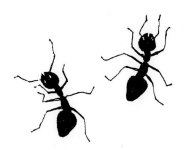

Bibliography

Australian Butterflies
Charles McCubbin
Thomas Nelson (1971)

Australian Orchids
Barbara Mullins/Margaret Martin
Angus and Robertson (1980)

Australian Rock and Tree Orchids
Densley Clyne
Landsdowne Press (1972)

Butterflies of Australia and New Zealand
Bernard D'Abrera
Five Mile Press (1984)

Complete Book of Australian Mammals
Edited by Ronald Strahan
Angus and Robertson (1983)

Encyclopaedia of Australian Plants
W. Roger Elliot/David L. Jones
Lothian Publishing, Vols. 1, 2, 3

Eucalypts
Stan Kelly
Thomas Nelson (1974)

Every Australian Bird Illustrated
Rigby (1975)

Hawks in Focus
Jack Cupper/Lindsay Cupper
Jaclin Enterprises Mildura (1981)

Our Arid Environment
Keith Davey
Reed Books (1983)

Patches of Australia, Deborah Brearley
Edward Arnold (1985)

Readers Digest Complete Book of Australian Birds
Readers Digest Publications (1976)

The Birds of Australia
Ken Simpson/Nicholas Day
Lloyd O'Neil Pty Ltd (1984)

What Animal is That?
Harry Frauca
Reed Books (1982)

What Wildflower is That?
Alec Blombery
Paul Hamlyn (1972)

The reader will find these references invaluable when working on a quilt or the like. They will provide a ready reference for colour and fabric selection when planning a piece of work.